YOUR RUGGED

BRUCE ALLYN FINDLAY

ESTHER BLAIR FINDLAY

Illustrations by

RICHARD DAWSON

AMERICAN IDEALS SERIES • • •

CONSTITUTION

*How America's House of Freedom
Is Planned and Built*

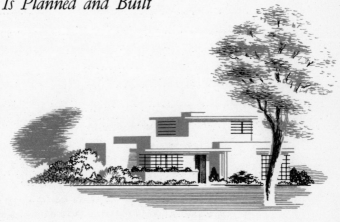

· STANFORD UNIVERSITY PRESS

ACKNOWLEDGMENTS

For invaluable criticisms, comments, and suggestions, the authors wish to thank Elizabeth Solem Dutton, Eugene Harley, Richard Dawson, Paul R. Murray, James Mussatti, Paul Cox, George Wakefield, Ray Brown, Edria Wallis, John C. Almack, A. John Bartky, Harry William Porter, Gordon B. and Allan H. Crary, and the staff of Stanford University Press.

CONTENTS

FOUNDATION LAID

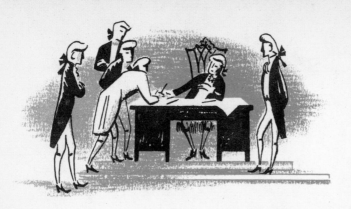

A House of Freedom for the United States had been started in 1781, under plans called the Articles of Confederation. But the structure showed increasing signs of weakness. So, throughout the summer of 1787, a group of delegates from all over the new nation met at Independence Hall in Philadelphia to see what could be done. Among them were George Washington, Benjamin Franklin, and James Madison. All were men of experience, leaders in their communities.

The purpose of the meeting was simply to revise the Articles of Confederation. But before long the delegates agreed that this would not be enough. They decided to dismantle the old structure and draw plans for a new one, using only those parts of the Articles which seemed sound and durable. After months of hard work and many compromises, they completed the new plans, signed them on September 17, 1787, and called them the Constitution of the United States. During the following year most of the states approved the plans. In April 1789, when George Washington became our first President, the actual building of the new government began.

The work done by the delegates who drafted the American Constitution has been praised throughout the world. With only a few formal changes, our House of Freedom stands today as these men planned it more than one hundred sixty years ago.

The most important difference between the old plans and the new ones lay in the basic idea of the sovereign power. Sovereign power means the power to establish and operate a government, and to change it if necessary. Under the Articles of Confederation, the sovereign power rested with the *states*, which had assigned a small part of their power to the central government. It was an imperfect league of friendship among thirteen semi-independent states. Instead of working together as a team, the states often pulled in different directions.

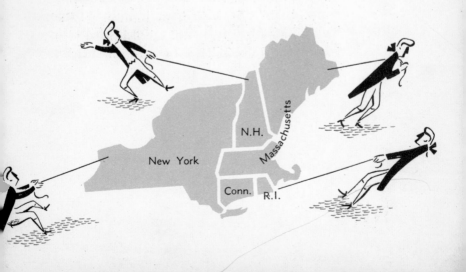

Under the Constitution, the sovereign power rests with the *people*, and the people alone. They grant some of this power to the central government, some to the states, and some they keep for themselves. Furthermore, the power they release is assigned only to officials who can be quickly turned out of office if they misuse or abuse their power.

The Constitution of the United States does four chief things. First, it sets up the framework of our government. Second, it points out what powers the government may exercise. Third, it places restrictions on the government. That is, it tells which powers the people are keeping for themselves. Fourth, it provides orderly methods by which the Constitution itself may be changed.

The government established by the Constitution has two main features. First, it is a federal system of government. That is, the power to govern is divided between the national government and the state governments. (The national government is often called the federal government.) Second, it is a government based

on the separation of powers. Whenever too
much power is concentrated in the hands of any
one person or a group of persons, tyranny and
dictatorship may arise. In the United States
government, power is divided among three
separate branches. These are called the legislative, executive, and judicial branches. Each of
them is constantly checking and balancing the
power of the others.

These important ideas and many others are
embodied in your Constitution—in the plans
for your House of Freedom.

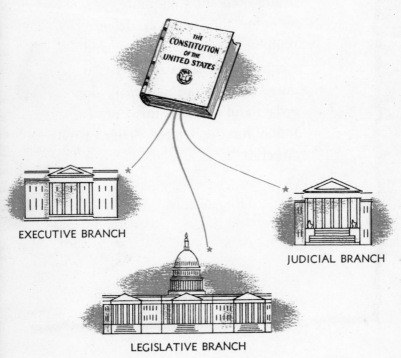

THE THREE BRANCHES OF
THE UNITED STATES GOVERNMENT

EXECUTIVE BRANCH

JUDICIAL BRANCH

LEGISLATIVE BRANCH

PREAMBLE

"We, the people of the United States, in order to form a more perfect Union, establish justice, insure domestic tranquility, provide for the common defense, promote the general welfare, and secure the blessings of liberty to ourselves and our posterity, do ordain and establish this Constitution for the United States of America."

"WE, THE PEOPLE
OF THE UNITED STATES,"

The Preamble states what *we, the people,* mean to accomplish with our government under the Constitution.

"IN ORDER TO FORM
A MORE PERFECT UNION"

Under the Articles of Confederation, the states had not been perfectly united. One aim of the new Constitution was to weld them into a Union which could not fall apart and which could carry out the duties assigned to it.

"ESTABLISH JUSTICE"

Our Constitution provides for a body of laws and a system of courts which make sure that each citizen will be treated justly and fairly.

"INSURE DOMESTIC TRANQUILITY"

Peace and order at home were of vital concern to the makers of our American Constitution. They are just as important today.

"PROVIDE FOR THE COMMON DEFENSE"

"PROMOTE THE GENERAL WELFARE"

"AND SECURE THE BLESSINGS OF LIBERTY
TO OURSELVES AND OUR POSTERITY"

"DO ORDAIN AND ESTABLISH
THIS CONSTITUTION FOR THE UNITED STATES
OF AMERICA"

CONSTRUCTION BEGUN

ARTICLE
I

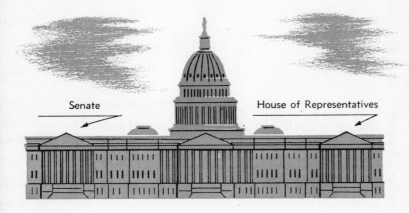

Senate

House of Representatives

THE CONGRESS
LEGISLATIVE BRANCH

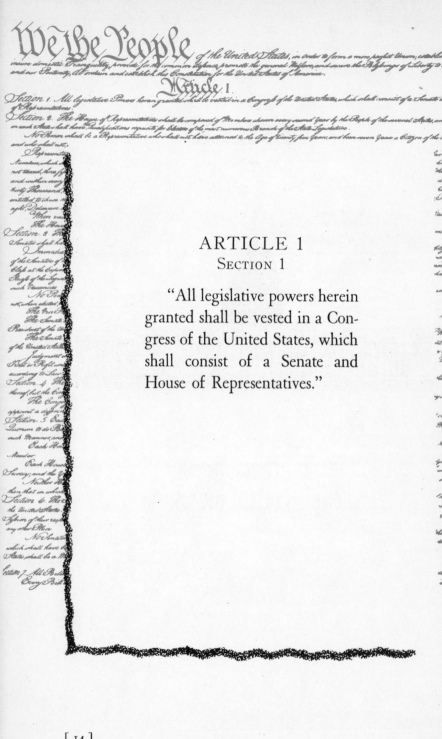

ARTICLE 1
SECTION 1

"All legislative powers herein granted shall be vested in a Congress of the United States, which shall consist of a Senate and House of Representatives."

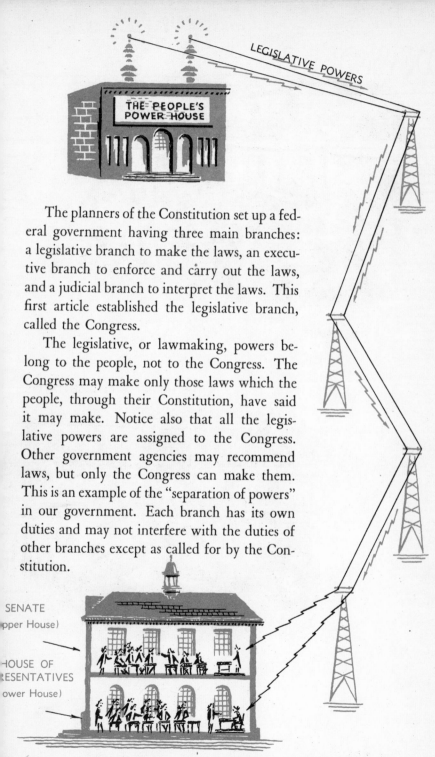

LEGISLATIVE POWERS

THE PEOPLE'S POWER HOUSE

The planners of the Constitution set up a federal government having three main branches: a legislative branch to make the laws, an executive branch to enforce and carry out the laws, and a judicial branch to interpret the laws. This first article established the legislative branch, called the Congress.

The legislative, or lawmaking, powers belong to the people, not to the Congress. The Congress may make only those laws which the people, through their Constitution, have said it may make. Notice also that all the legislative powers are assigned to the Congress. Other government agencies may recommend laws, but only the Congress can make them. This is an example of the "separation of powers" in our government. Each branch has its own duties and may not interfere with the duties of other branches except as called for by the Constitution.

SENATE
(Upper House)

HOUSE OF REPRESENTATIVES
(Lower House)

OLD CONGRESS HALL - 1790

THE SENATE

THE HOUSE OF REPRESENTATIVES

You give: (*a*) Authority to the Congress alone to make laws for the nation; (*b*) instructions that there shall always be two separate divisions in the Congress.

You get: (*a*) Laws which have been carefully thought out by Congressmen elected to represent you; (*b*) control of your Congressmen, since you vote them into office and can vote them out again; (*c*) two divisions of Congress which serve as a check on each other.

ARTICLE 1
SECTION 2
CLAUSE 1

"The House of Representatives shall be composed of members chosen every second year by the people of the several states, and the electors in each state shall have the qualifications requisite for electors of the most numerous branch of the State Legislature."

CLAUSE 2

"No person shall be a Representative who shall not have attained to the age of twenty-five years, and been seven years a citizen of the United States, and who shall not, when elected, be an inhabitant of that state in which he shall be chosen."

The makers of the Constitution wanted the House of Representatives to represent as many voters as possible—that is, they wanted it to be popularly elected. But it was hopeless to unscramble the different voting rules then in force in the states. They left voting rules to the states, therefore, except to say that anyone could vote for a national Representative who was allowed, in his own state, to vote for members of "the most numerous branch of the State Legislature." In most states, the branch having the greater number of members was popularly elected.

In a further effort to keep the House of Representatives close to the people, the Constitution directed that no Representative could serve for more than two years without being re-elected.

Your Representative

QUALIFICATIONS FOR REPRESENTATIVE

1. At least twenty-five years old.
2. A citizen of the United States for at least seven years.
3. A resident of the state which elects him.

You give: Qualifications strict enough to call forth experienced candidates, but not so strict as to block the will of the people.

You get: Representatives, both young and old, who have been citizens of the United States long enough to understand its needs, and who are familiar with the states they represent.

[19]

ARTICLE 1
SECTION 2
CLAUSE 3

"Representatives and direct taxes shall be apportioned among the several states which may be included within this Union, according to their respective numbers, ~~which shall be determined by adding to the whole number of free persons, including those bound to service for a term of years, and excluding Indians not taxed, three fifths of all other persons.~~ The actual enumeration shall be made within three years after the first meeting of the Congress of the United States, and within every subsequent term of ten years, in such manner as they shall by law direct. The number of Representatives shall not exceed one for every thirty thousand, but each state shall have at least one Representative; ~~and until such enumeration shall be made, the state of New Hampshire shall be entitled to choose 3; Massachusetts, 8; Rhode Island and Providence Plantations, 1; Connecticut, 5; New York, 6; New Jersey, 4; Pennsylvania, 8; Delaware, 1; Maryland, 6; Virginia, 10; North Carolina, 5; South Carolina, 5; and Georgia, 3.~~"

Some parts of the Constitution are no longer in effect. In this book, these parts are marked out by light lines.

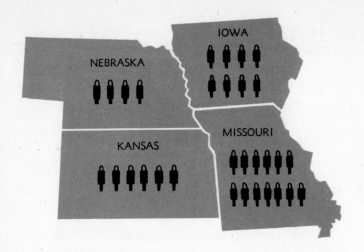

This clause introduces the "Great Compromise" of the Constitutional Convention. The larger states, led by Virginia, wanted a Congress of two houses in which the total number of Congressmen would be divided among the states according to their population. The smaller states, led by New Jersey, demanded that each state, regardless of size, have an equal number of Congressmen. After long and bitter argument, a compromise was reached. It was agreed that each state would be represented in the House of Representatives according to its population, as stated in this clause. And it was agreed that each state, regardless of size, would be represented in the Senate by two Senators (see page 28). Since the Senate must agree to all laws, the smaller states were satisfied.

To avoid disputes over the number of Representatives a state might send to Congress, the Constitution directed that an enumeration, or census, should be taken every ten years to see how many people were living in each state. A law now requires that the states be told after each census just how many Representatives they are entitled to.

The makers of the Constitution intended that there should be one Representative in Congress for every 30,000 people. But as the country expanded and the population grew, it became clear that the House would become too large for efficient work. In 1929, therefore, a law was passed that limits the total number of Representatives to 435.

You can find out the approximate number of Representatives for each state in this way: (1) Divide 435 into the total population of the United States according to the latest census. The answer is the number of people that each Representative stands for. In recent years it has been

over 300,000 people. (2) Divide your answer into the number of people in each state according to the latest census. That tells you how many Representatives each state should have. If any state has fewer people than the average Representative stands for, that state is still entitled to one Representative.

Direct taxes are paid directly by the individual to the government. (For the differences between direct and indirect taxes, see page 65.) Direct taxes must be divided among the states in the same way that Representatives are divided.

John Q. Citizen

No one is "bound to service" in the United States today. Indians are now citizens. The phrase "three-fifths of all other persons" referred to Negro slaves. The Fourteenth Amendment established their citizenship and included them fully in the census count (page 228).

You give: (a) A formula which distributes membership in the House of Representatives among the states according to their population; (b) instructions that the people are to be counted every ten years.

You get: A House of Representatives (a) which is elected directly by the people; (b) in which each state has influence in proportion to its population.

ARTICLE 1
SECTION 2
CLAUSE 4

"When vacancies happen in the representation from any state, the executive authority thereof shall issue writs of election to fill such vacancies."

CLAUSE 5

"The House of Representatives shall choose their Speaker and other officers; and shall have the sole power of impeachment."

[24]

When a Representative dies or resigns, the Governor of his state calls a special election to replace him, unless a regular election is about to occur. The Governor may not appoint a successor, as he may when a seat in the Senate becomes vacant (see page 30).

The Speaker of the House of Representatives is a very important person. He presides at all meetings of the House, and carries out other duties which are outlined in the rules of the House. He is the leader of the majority party— that is, of the political party having the largest number of members in the House. Also, if both President and Vice-President should die, he would become President.

Other officers of the House of Representatives are: Clerk, Sergeant at Arms, Chaplain, Postmaster, and Doorkeeper.

President   Vice-President   Speaker of the House

Order of Presidential Succession

You give: Authority to the House of Representatives to choose its own Speaker and other officers.

You get: An able leader of the House who is also qualified to lead the nation if both President and Vice-President should die.

"Sole power of impeachment" means, in terms of the Constitution, the right of the House of Representatives, alone, to accuse a high civil officer of the government with some important crime. Such crimes are "treason, bribery, or other high crimes or misdemeanors" (see page 141). In other words, whenever a high govern-

Speaker

Members of the
House of Representatives

Clerk

IMPEACHMENT CHARGES

ment official abuses the trust you have placed in
him, the House, elected directly by you every
two years, can bring charges against him.

When the House has worked out its charges,
it brings them before the Senate (see page 39),
and acts as the prosecutor. The Senate, in turn,
acts as judge and jury in the case.

You give: Responsibility to the House to watch the actions
of high government officials, along with the
power to accuse them if they betray your trust.

You get: Protection against dishonesty and other criminal
actions in important government offices.

[27]

ARTICLE 1
SECTION 3
CLAUSE 1

"The Senate of the United States shall be composed of two Senators from each state, ~~chosen by the Legislature thereof~~,* for six years; and each Senator shall have one vote."

* Amendment 17 provides for direct election of Senators (see page 240).

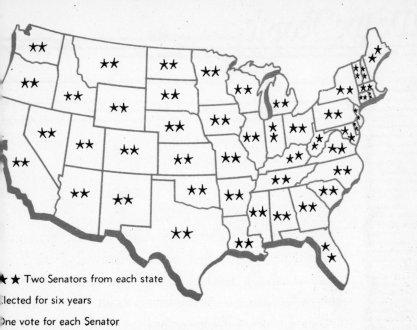

★ ★ Two Senators from each state

Elected for six years

One vote for each Senator

This clause is another portion of the "Great Compromise" (see page 21). Every state, no matter how small, elects two Senators to guard its interests. For example, the northeastern part of the country, heavily populated, sends so many Representatives to Congress that the House might pass laws that would be unfair to the sparsely settled Southwest. But each state in the Southwest has two Senators in Congress to resist such laws.

You give: Each state the right to elect two members of the Senate, who serve six-year terms.

You get: Equal representation in the Senate, which serves as a check against domination of smaller states by larger ones, or of thinly settled regions by populous ones.

ARTICLE 1
Section 3
Clause 2

"Immediately after they shall be assembled in consequence of the first election, they shall be divided as equally as may be into three classes. ~~The seats of the Senators of the first class shall be vacated at the expiration of the second year, of the second class at the expiration of the fourth year, and of the third class at the expiration of the sixth year,~~ so that one-third may be chosen every second year; and if vacancies happen by resignation, or otherwise, during the recess of the Legislature of any state, the Executive thereof may make temporary appointments until the next meeting of the Legislature, which shall then fill such vacancies."*

* Amendment 17 changes this method of filling vacancies.

The six-year terms of one-third of the Senators expire every two years, when their seats must be filled by elections. Two-thirds of the members are "carried over." Thus, the Senate is sometimes called "the House that never dies."

You give: The people an opportunity to elect one-third of the Senate every two years.

You get: A continuous and experienced Senate, yet one whose actions are surveyed by the public every two years.

ARTICLE 1
Section 3
Clause 3

"No person shall be a Senator who shall not have attained to the age of thirty years, and been nine years a citizen of the United States, and who shall not, when elected, be an inhabitant of that state for which he shall be chosen."

QUALIFICATIONS FOR SENATOR

1. At least thirty years of age.
2. A citizen of the United States for nine years.
3. A citizen of the state he represents.

You give: A list of qualifications for Senators even more strict than those required for Representatives.

You get: Mature, experienced Senators who are familiar with the affairs of the nation and of their states.

ARTICLE 1
SECTION 3
CLAUSE 4

"The Vice-President of the United States shall be president of the Senate, but shall have no vote, unless they be equally divided."

President of the Senate
(Vice-President of the U.S.)

"The vote is a tie, Mr. President. How do you vote?"

Clerk

This is the only specific obligation assigned by the Constitution to the Vice-President. It is an important one, however, even though the Vice-President rarely votes on laws. As president of the Senate, he keeps his eye on appointments, treaties, new legislation, and other things which he must understand if he should suddenly become President of the United States.

So that he may be even better informed, he is usually invited now to meet with the President's Cabinet.

You give: The Vice-President an important post as president of the Senate, with the opportunity to keep well informed about the affairs of the nation.

You get: As president of the Senate, a man who has been elected by the people.

[35]

ARTICLE 1
SECTION 3
CLAUSE 5

"The Senate shall choose their other officers, and also a President pro tempore,* in the absence of the Vice-President, or when he shall exercise the office of President of the United States."

* "Pro tempore" is a Latin phrase which means "for the time being."

OFFICERS
OF THE SENATE

President
    Pro Tempore .. *[signature]*

Secretary · · · *[signature]*

Sergeant at Arms .. *[signature]*

Chaplain · · · · *[signature]*

Secretary
    to the Majority .. *[signature]*

Secretary
    to the Minority .. *[signature]*

ARTICLE 1
Section 3
Clause 6

"The Senate shall have the sole power to try all impeachments. When sitting for that purpose, they shall be on oath or affirmation. When the President of the United States is tried, the Chief Justice shall preside; and no person shall be convicted without the concurrence of two-thirds of the members present."

The House of Representatives formulates the charge (see page 26). The Senate, alone, decides whether the accused official is innocent or guilty. Since impeachment charges are very serious, the Constitution provides that two-thirds of the Senators present must agree to a conviction.

You give: Responsibility to the Senate to decide whether or not high government officials have betrayed their trust.

You get: (*a*) Serious, mature, and firm judgments from the Senate after the House has made its accusations; (*b*) the Chief Justice of the United States as an unbiased presiding officer when the President is tried.

ARTICLE 1
Section 3
Clause 7

"Judgment in cases of impeachment shall not extend further than to removal from office, and disqualification to hold and enjoy any office of honor, trust, or profit under the United States: but the party convicted shall nevertheless be liable and subject to indictment, trial, judgment, and punishment, according to law."

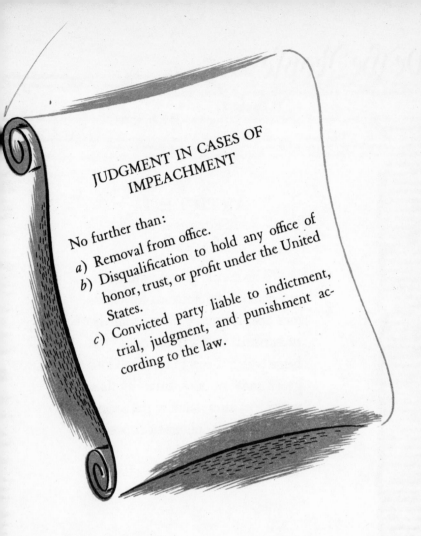

JUDGMENT IN CASES OF IMPEACHMENT

No further than:
a) Removal from office.
b) Disqualification to hold any office of honor, trust, or profit under the United States.
c) Convicted party liable to indictment, trial, judgment, and punishment according to the law.

You give: Limitations to the penalties which may be imposed by the Senate against persons impeached, but you make such persons subject to the regular procedure of the courts.

You get: Protection of officials from severe punishments until their cases have been tried according to usual court procedures.

ARTICLE 1
Section 4
Clause 1

"The times, places, and manner of holding elections for Senators and Representatives shall be prescribed in each state by the Legislature thereof; but the Congress may at any time by law make or alter such regulations, except as to the places of choosing Senators."

With one exception, all states hold Congressional elections on the Tuesday after the first Monday in November of even-numbered years (1952, 1954, and so on). Maine holds its elections in September.

Election regulations in general are left to the states, but Congress has passed certain laws from time to time to safeguard the honesty and fairness of national elections. One law requires that secret ballots be used. Another law limits the amount of money that candidates for the Senate and the House of Representatives may spend during campaigns for election.

ARTICLE 1
Section 4
Clause 2

"The Congress shall assemble at least once in every year, ~~and such meeting shall be on the first Monday in December,~~ unless they shall by law appoint a different day."

New Congress meets
in <u>odd</u>-numbered years

Kings or their appointees had sometimes forbidden legislatures to assemble or had refused to call them into session. With this clause, the makers of the Constitution made certain that this would not happen under our government, and they also saw to it that Congress would keep on the job.

Amendment 20 (see page 246) provides that the new Congress shall meet on January 3 of the odd-numbered years following the regular November elections. Congress also meets on January 3 of the even-numbered years. Sessions last as long as there is work to be done. Also, the President has power to call Congress into special session if necessary (see page 136).

ARTICLE 1
SECTION 5
CLAUSE 1

"Each house shall be the judge of the elections, returns, and qualifications of its own members, and a majority of each shall constitute a quorum to do business; but a smaller number may adjourn from day to day, and may be authorized to compel the attendance of absent members in such manner and under such penalties as each house may provide."

Returns and Qualifications

Returns and Qualifications

ARTICLE 1
SECTION 5
CLAUSE 2

"Each house may determine the rules of its proceedings, punish its members for disorderly behavior, and, with the concurrence of two-thirds, expel a member."

CLAUSE 3

"Each house shall keep a journal of its proceedings, and from time to time publish the same, excepting such parts as may in their judgment require secrecy; and the yeas and nays of the members of either house on any question shall, at the desire of one-fifth of those present, be entered on the journal."

CLAUSE 4

"Neither house, during the session of Congress, shall, without the consent of the other, adjourn for more than three days, nor to any other place than that in which the two houses shall be sitting."

You give: Your Congress (*a*) the right to judge the eligibility of its members; (*b*) further instructions about keeping on the job; (*c*) authority to make its own rules and regulations.

You get: (*a*) Congressmen qualified to be members, for if either house declares a person not eligible for membership, there are ways to exclude him; (*b*) assurance that the work of Congress will not be delayed through absences; (*c*) a complete record of events in Congress for the public to review; (*d*) knowledge of how your Congressmen vote on important questions.

ARTICLE 1
Section 6
Clause 1

"The Senators and Representatives shall receive a compensation for their services, to be ascertained by law, and paid out of the Treasury of the United States. They shall in all cases, except treason, felony, and breach of the peace, be privileged from arrest during their attendance at the session of their respective houses, and in going to and returning from the same; and for any speech or debate in either house they shall not be questioned in any other place."

You give: Your Congressmen (*a*) salaries, expenses, free postage, and other compensations; (*b*) freedom from arrest for ordinary reasons while doing their work; (*c*) freedom from arrest for anything they may say in Congress.

You get: A fearless expression of the thoughts of your Congressman that he could not risk if he were liable to be arrested for slander, libel, or other causes.

ARTICLE 1
Section 6
Clause 2

"No Senator or Representative shall, during the time for which he was elected, be appointed to any civil office under the authority of the United States, which shall have been created, or the emoluments whereof shall have been increased during such time; and no person holding any office under the United States shall be a member of either house during his continuance in office."

You give: Instructions (*a*) that prevent a Congressman from holding any job which he may have helped to create or whose salary has been increased during his time in office; (*b*) that require government officeholders to resign their positions before becoming Congressmen.

You get: Protection from (*a*) the creation by Congress of high-salaried positions for its own members; (*b*) undue influence by Congress on the other branches of the government.

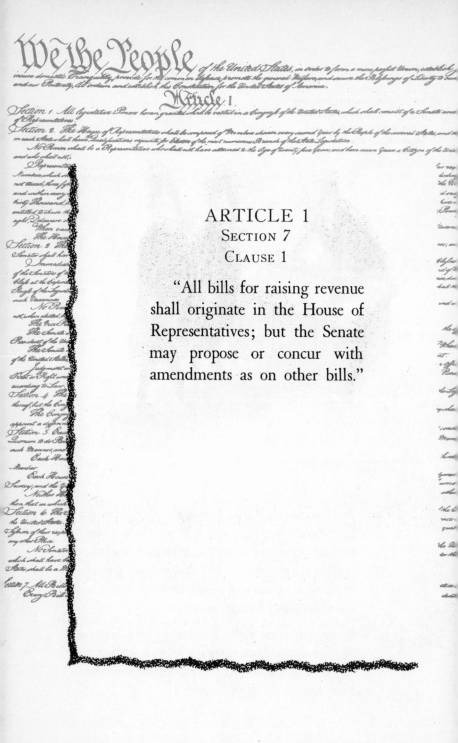

ARTICLE 1
SECTION 7
CLAUSE 1

"All bills for raising revenue shall originate in the House of Representatives; but the Senate may propose or concur with amendments as on other bills."

Representative

Tax Bills

Senators

You give: To the House of Representatives, most directly representing the people, the right to originate all bills intended to raise money by taxation.

You get: The opportunity every two years to vote your Congressman out of office if he doesn't handle tax bills as you think he should.

[55]

ARTICLE 1
SECTION 7
CLAUSE 2

"Every bill which shall have passed the House of Representatives and the Senate, shall, before it becomes a law, be presented to the President of the United States; . . . ."

". . . . if he approve, he shall sign it, but if not, he shall return it, with his objections, to that house in which it shall have originated, ..."

From Congress

Back to Congress

"Veto" is a Latin word meaning "I forbid."

". . . . who shall enter the objections at large on their journal, and proceed to reconsider it."

"If after such reconsideration two-thirds of that house shall agree to pass the bill, it shall be sent, together with the objections, to the other house, by which it shall likewise be reconsidered, and if approved by two-thirds of that house, it shall become a law. But in all such cases the votes of both houses shall be determined by yeas and nays, and the names of the persons voting for and against the bill shall be entered on the journal of each house respectively."

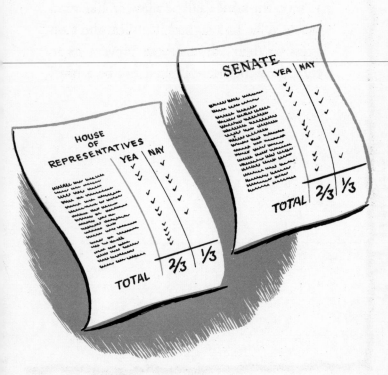

"If any bill shall not be returned by the President within ten days (Sundays excepted) after it shall have been presented to him, the same shall be a law, in like manner as if he had signed it, unless the Congress by their adjournment prevent its return, in which case it shall not be a law."

A bill becomes
a law unless it
is vetoed within
ten days

You give: (*a*) To the President the right to approve or disapprove all bills; (*b*) to Congress the responsibility of mustering two-thirds of its members in favor of any bill of which the President disapproves before that bill can become law.

You get· (*a*) Checks and balances between both houses of Congress and between Congress and the President; (*b*) protection against hasty and illconsidered action either by Congress or by the President.

ARTICLE 1
Section 7
Clause 3

"Every order, resolution, or vote to which the concurrence of the Senate and House of Representatives may be necessary (except on a question of adjournment) shal be presented to the President of the United States; and before the same shall take effect, shall be approved by him, or being disapproved by him, shall be repassed by two-thirds of the Senate and the House of Representatives, according to the rules and limitations prescribed in the case of a bill."

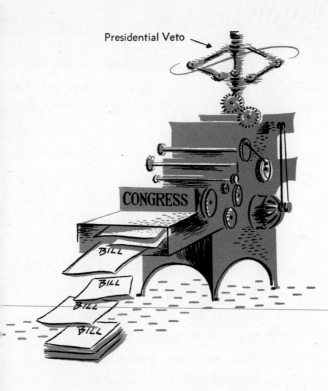

Presidential Veto

Some machines have "governors" to keep them from going too fast. The presidential veto is the "governor" on the lawmaking machinery of the United States government. It prevents too hasty action by Congress.

You give: To the President the responsibility of signing or vetoing all measures, not only bills, that have been passed by both houses of Congress.

You get: Another important check and balance in the process of lawmaking.

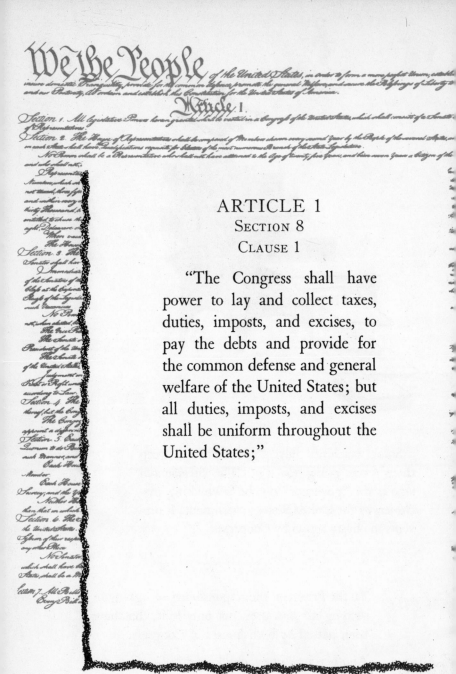

ARTICLE 1
SECTION 8
CLAUSE 1

"The Congress shall have power to lay and collect taxes, duties, imposts, and excises, to pay the debts and provide for the common defense and general welfare of the United States; but all duties, imposts, and excises shall be uniform throughout the United States;"

Section 8 of Article 1 assigns certain powers and functions to Congress. You have already read of the limitation upon its power to levy direct taxes (page 23). Here, Congress is granted the general power to collect taxes.

Among the indirect taxes which Congress may levy are *duties* and *imposts* on goods imported from foreign countries, and *excises*, which are taxes on the manufacture and sale of many articles within the country, on certain business transactions, and so on. An indirect tax, unlike a direct tax, may be passed along from one person to another. A manufacturer pays his tax to the government, but adds that amount to the price of his product. The wholesaler, in turn, adds his indirect taxes, and passes the total cost along to the retailer. And so on, until the whole tax bill is finally paid by you, the consumer.

Congress may use its taxing powers —

TO PAY THE DEBTS

AND PROVIDE FOR THE COMMON DEFENSE

AND GENERAL WELFARE OF THE UNITED STATES

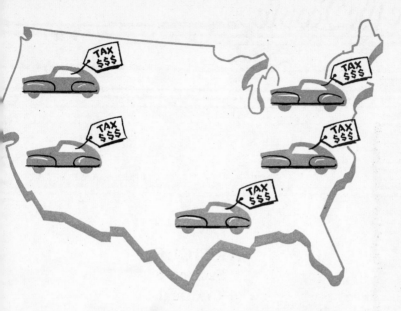

"... BUT ALL DUTIES, IMPOSTS, AND EX-
CISES SHALL BE UNIFORM THROUGHOUT
THE UNITED STATES."

Indirect taxes must be the same throughout
the country. A federal tax on automobiles, for
example, or on theater tickets, tobacco, or cos-
metics, shall be the same in San Francisco as in
New York and New Orleans.

You give: Power to Congress to collect the money required: (*a*) to protect the nation against enemies abroad; (*b*) to take care of the needs of
the country at home.

You get: (*a*) A federal government strong enough to do,
and to pay for, the things it is authorized by the
Constitution to do; (*b*) a fair and uniform system of taxation.

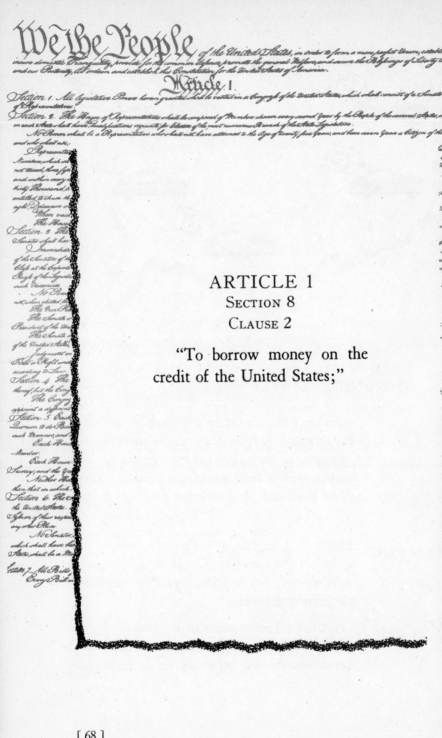

ARTICLE 1
SECTION 8
CLAUSE 2

"To borrow money on the credit of the United States;"

You give: (*a*) Power to Congress to borrow money, mainly from its citizens, as needed to carry on the affairs of government; (*b*) part of your taxes to pay back the money, with interest, that your government borrows.

You get: (*a*) The services and protection of your government; (*b*) interest on money you lend to the government.

ARTICLE 1
SECTION 8
CLAUSE 3

"To regulate commerce with foreign nations, ..."

". . . . and among the several states, and with the Indian tribes;"

The first part of this brief clause gives Congress complete and exclusive control over international commerce. Using this authority, Congress has passed laws governing (1) goods entering or leaving the country, (2) ships and other means of transportation and communication, and (3) the people who can be admitted to the United States.

Under this broad power, our commercial relations with other countries are kept uniform, which helps to avoid international complications. Also, states with important seaports are prevented from taxing the commerce of other states.

You give: To the Congress complete control over foreign commerce, which includes the following authority: (*a*) to collect tariffs on imported goods; (*b*) to forbid import of diseased foods and other undesirable products; (*c*) to control immigration; (*d*) to prevent export of materials needed at home; (*e*) to encourage and help navigation.

You get: (*a*) Government revenue, and protection of home industries; (*b*) safeguards to health and morals; (*c*) protection from too much immigration and from undesirable aliens; (*d*) conservation of natural resources; (*e*) operation of lighthouses, dredging of harbors and rivers, and other aids to shipping; (*f*) uniform regulation of international trade in the interest of the nation as a whole.

Regulation of interstate commerce, which is granted in the second part of Clause 3, is one of the most important powers assigned to Congress. Along with the taxing power, it has enabled our country to adapt itself to the change from a simple agricultural nation to a complex industrial one. Under these powers, important economic problems can be handled on a national scale.

"To regulate" is the broad power to make rules for carrying on commerce. Interstate commerce includes (1) all the things which move among the states, including goods, persons, and words; (2) the means by which they move, including railroads, ships, telegraph wires, express companies, and navigable rivers. "Among the several states" refers to any movement from one state to another or through another. It also includes things that are done wholly in one state but are nevertheless a step in interstate commerce—for example, iron ore that is mined in Wisconsin for use in Illinois steel mills.

In addition to granting this power to Congress, this clause also restricts the states. Any state law or tax may be declared unconstitutional if it interferes with interstate commerce or the regulation of that commerce by Congress.

You give: To Congress authority: (*a*) to regulate interstate commerce; (*b*) to supervise trade with the Indians.

You get: (*a*) Free flow of goods among the states without tariffs; (*b*) encouragement and supervision of transportation by water, land, and air; (*c*) a check on the movement of harmful goods or persons; (*d*) protection of Indians from exploitation.

ARTICLE 1
SECTION 8
CLAUSE 4

"To establish a uniform rule of naturalization, ..."

". . . . and uniform laws on the subject of bankruptcies throughout the United States;"

You give: To Congress authority to pass laws which describe how foreign-born persons may become citizens of the United States.

You get: Citizenship for persons who merit that privilege, and rejection of those who do not.

You give: To Congress the power to pass laws which protect an individual if he is in debt beyond his ability to pay.

You get: (*a*) Protection from utter poverty if you fall into serious debt; (*b*) a fair share of a debtor's assets if you are one of his creditors.

ARTICLE 1
SECTION 8
CLAUSE 5

"To coin money, regulate the value thereof, and of foreign coin,* . . . ."

* This phrase was important in the early years of our country, when foreign money was common and United States money was still scarce.

". . . . and fix the standard of weights and measures;"

You give: To Congress authority to produce money (of metal or paper) and to determine its worth.

You get: Money that has the same appearance and value throughout the country.

You give: Authority to Congress to standardize weights and measures.

You get: Assurance, for example, that a pound will be the same weight and a mile the same length everywhere in the country.

ARTICLE 1
Section 8
Clause 6

"To provide for the punishment of counterfeiting the securities and current coin of the United
States;"

Clause 7

"To establish post offices and
post roads;"

You give: Power to Congress to punish people who make or distribute counterfeit money, false government bonds, and the like.

You get: A government service which safeguards the value of your money and securities.

You give: To Congress the authority (*a*) to set up and operate a complete system for handling mail; (*b*) to assist in developing the land, water, and air routes over which the mail is hauled.

You get: (*a*) Uniform postage rates; (*b*) national distribution of mail at a bargain; (*c*) better systems of transportation and communication.

ARTICLE 1
SECTION 8
CLAUSE 8

"To promote the progress of science and useful arts, by securing for limited times to authors and inventors the exclusive right to their respective writings and discoveries;"

You give: To Congress authority to pass laws which give to inventors, authors, and artists, for a limited number of years, exclusive right to make and sell the things they create.

You get: (*a*) An opportunity to use and enjoy the many things created by American inventors and artists; (*b*) the privilege of enjoying the money and fame that may come from anything you invent or create.

We the People of the United States, in order to form a more perfect Union, establish insure domestic Tranquility, provide for the common defence, promote the general Welfare, and secure the Blessings of Liberty to and our Posterity, do ordain and establish this Constitution for the United States of America.

Article I

Section 1. All legislative Powers herein granted shall be vested in a Congress of the United States, which shall consist of a Senate and of Representatives.

Section 2. The House of Representatives shall be composed of Members chosen every second Year by the People of the several States, and in each State shall have Qualifications requisite for Electors of the most numerous Branch of the State Legislature.

No Person shall be a Representative who shall not have attained to the Age of twenty-five Years, and been seven Years a Citizen of the and who shall not,

ARTICLE 1
SECTION 8
CLAUSE 9

"To constitute tribunals inferior to the Supreme Court;"

CLAUSE 10

"To define and punish piracies and felonies committed on the high seas, and offenses against the law of nations;"

You give: Authority to Congress to establish federal courts below the level of the Supreme Court. (For information about the Supreme Court, see page 145.)

You get: A system of federal courts adaptable to the population and territory of the United States (see also page 148).

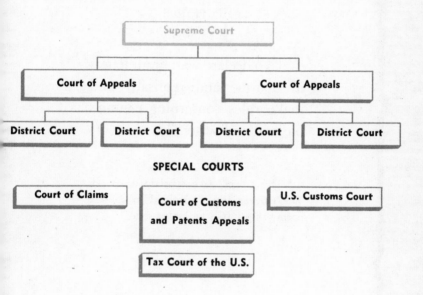

You give: Power to Congress to reach outside the territory of the United States in order to fulfill its obligation to maintain law and order.

You get: (*a*) Protection for citizens and ships of the United States abroad; (*b*) supervision of the actions of United States citizens abroad; (*c*) protection against disputes with foreign nations as a result of actions by private citizens.

ARTICLE 1
SECTION 8
CLAUSE 11

"To declare war, grant letters of marque and reprisal,* and make rules concerning captures on land and water;"

* This power was important when private citizens were permitted to capture enemy ships. It is no longer used.

[84]

War is the most fateful action that a nation can undertake. With this clause, the people state that only Congress may declare war formally. However, war may be started by a foreign power, as when Japan attacked Hawaii in 1941. Or, the President, as commander in chief of the armed forces, may decide that it is necessary, in order to protect our interests, to use armed force. Congress may then meet to declare "that a state of war exists."

You give: Authority to the Congress (*a*) to declare war; (*b*) to set up rules for the capture of enemy property, or the property of neutral countries assisting the enemy.

You get: Assurance that after studying the facts, Congress, and only Congress, may declare war.

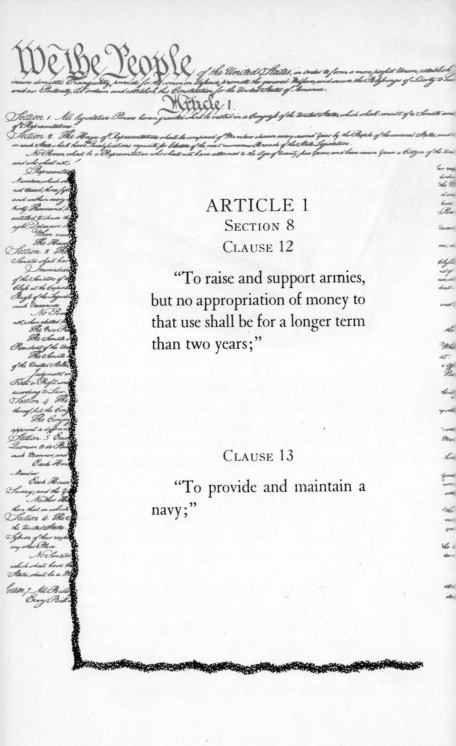

ARTICLE 1
Section 8
Clause 12

"To raise and support armies, but no appropriation of money to that use shall be for a longer term than two years;"

Clause 13

"To provide and maintain a navy;"

MONEY
FOR
ARMIES

FOR TWO YEARS ONLY

These clauses grant immense military power. Congress can draft citizens into the armed forces and require them to obey military law. It can buy food, clothing, arms, trucks, and all the other requirements of the armed forces. But the makers of the Constitution were determined that the military establishment should be held under continual control of the Congress. They stated, therefore, that money for armies should not be appropriated for longer than two years at a time. Actually, Congress makes new appropriations every year.

You give: Authority to Congress to raise armies and pay for them, and to conduct total war.

You get: Assurance (*a*) that armies will be available when needed; (*b*) that the armed forces will be controlled by your Representatives.

You give: To Congress authority to maintain the Navy.

You get: A navy in continuous operation, ready to protect the nation when necessary.

ARTICLE 1
SECTION 8
CLAUSE 14

"To make rules for the government and regulation of the land and naval forces;"

CLAUSE 15

"To provide for calling forth the militia to execute the laws of the Union, suppress insurrections, and repel invasions;"

CLAUSE 16

"To provide for organizing, arming, and disciplining the militia, and for governing such part of them as may be employed in the service of the United States, reserving to the states, respectively, the appointment of the officers, and the authority of training the militia according to the discipline prescribed by Congress;"

The organized militia of the states are now
known as the National Guard. The federal government now pays most of the expenses for their
training and equipment. It can absorb them into
the United States Army in time of war, or use
them to maintain law and order at other times.

You give: To Congress the power to keep the National
Guard trained and equipped for emergencies.

You get: A group of citizens in training to add to the
regular Army when needed.

ARTICLE 1
SECTION 8
CLAUSE 17

"To exercise exclusive legislation in all cases whatsoever over such district (not exceeding ten miles square) as may, by cession of particular states and the acceptance of Congress, become the seat of government of the United States, and to exercise like authority over all places purchased by the consent of the Legislature of the state in which the same shall be, for the erection of forts, magazines, arsenals, dockyards, and other needful buildings;—And"

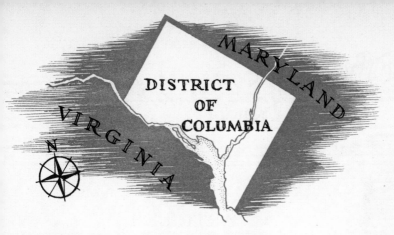

The first part of this clause refers to the District of Columbia, the seat of our national government. Washington, D.C. (the District of Columbia), is governed by Congress, and its affairs are administered by a board of three commissioners, appointed by the President with the consent of the Senate.

The United States government is the greatest landowner in the nation. It owns parks, forests, military posts, courthouses, post offices, and many other properties throughout the country.

You give: To Congress the authority to buy and control whatever property the national government needs to carry out its duties.

You get: The use of parks, post offices, and many other services that are available as a result of property owned and operated by your government.

ARTICLE 1
SECTION 8
CLAUSE 18

"To make all laws which shall be necessary and proper for carrying into execution the foregoing powers, and all other powers vested by this Constitution in the government of the United States, or in any department or officer thereof."

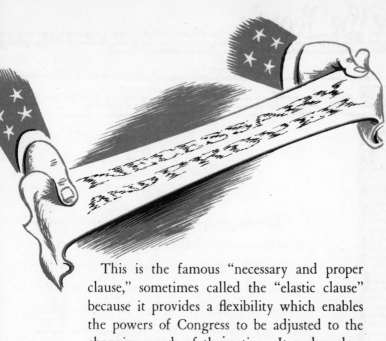

This is the famous "necessary and proper clause," sometimes called the "elastic clause" because it provides a flexibility which enables the powers of Congress to be adjusted to the changing needs of the nation. It makes clear that Congress can use various means to carry out its delegated powers. For example, the power of Congress to regulate foreign and interstate commerce implies that Congress may improve rivers and harbors to aid commerce. This clause makes it certain that such means may be used unless the Supreme Court rules that they are not "necessary and proper" to the delegated power.

You give: Power to Congress to make such laws as may be necessary and proper for the government to carry out the duties assigned to it in the Constitution.

You get: Assurance that the government can operate from day to day in the ways that you have designated.

ARTICLE 1
SECTION 9
CLAUSE 1

"The migration or importation of such persons as any of the states now existing shall think proper to admit shall not be prohibited by the Congress prior to the year one thousand eight hundred and eight, but a tax or duty may be imposed on such importation, not exceeding ten dollars for each person."*

* This clause referred to the slave trade. It was a restriction, until the year 1808, on the power of Congress to regulate foreign trade.

CLAUSE 2

"The privilege of the writ of habeas corpus shall not be suspended, unless when in cases of rebellion or invasion the public safety may require it."

Clause 2 means that a person cannot be held in prison without charges being made against him. Dictatorial governments have often used such methods to do away with people who disagreed with the government. (The words "habeas corpus" are the opening words of a Latin sentence which means that the prisoner must be brought before the court.)

You deny: To the government any right to put people in jail and to hold them there without bringing charges, except in times of severe emergency.

You get: Protection from being jailed and held there without explanation or reason.

ARTICLE 1
Section 9
Clause 3

"No bill of attainder or ex post facto law shall be passed."

"But I haven't had a trial!"

"You don't get a trial. The Legislature has already passed a bill of attainder that convicts you!"

A bill of attainder is an act passed by a legislature to punish a person without a regular trial in court. It is another means sometimes used by dictatorial governments to deal with persons who oppose them.

"Ex post facto" is a Latin phrase meaning "after the deed." Under this clause, if a law is passed today, it may not be used to convict a person for some act that he committed yesterday.

You deny: To Congress any right (*a*) to punish a person without a fair trial; (*b*) to declare any act a crime that was not a crime at the time the act was committed.

You get: Assurance (*a*) that no one will receive punishment by a legislative act; (*b*) that if you know what the law is and obey it, you can never be convicted of a crime.

ARTICLE 1
Section 9
Clause 4

"No capitation or other direct tax shall be laid, unless in proportion to the census or enumeration herein before directed to be taken."

Article 1, Section 2, Clause 3, states that direct taxes shall be apportioned among the states according to their population. This clause underlines the earlier one by saying that direct taxes shall not be levied by Congress in any other way.

A capitation tax is levied equally against each person in all of the states. Taxes levied against land or buildings are also direct. Congress has seldom levied direct taxes because in some ways they are unfair and because they strike directly at the citizen's pocketbook, which makes them unpopular politically. A tax on incomes is a direct tax from one viewpoint, but an indirect tax from another viewpoint. In 1913, Amendment 16 was added to the Constitution to establish the right of Congress to tax incomes (see page 238).

ARTICLE 1
SECTION 9
CLAUSE 5

"No tax or duty shall be laid on articles exported from any state."

CLAUSE 6

"No preference shall be given by any regulation of commerce or revenue to the ports of one state over those of another; nor shall vessels bound to, or from, one state be obliged to enter, clear, or pay duties to another."

This clause prevents Congress from penalizing any state by taxing her exports. It also encourages our manufacturers and farmers to trade abroad.

You deny: To Congress any power to levy taxes on goods being shipped out of the country.

You get: Benefits of world trade.

The first part of this clause forbids Congress to pass any laws that would directly favor the trade of one state over another. But it does not mean, for example, that every harbor in the nation must be dredged whenever one of them is dredged.

Under the Constitution the states gave up their control over interstate and foreign trade. The second part of this clause protects the rights of the states from abuse by the powers they surrendered.

You deny: To Congress any right to give advantages in shipping to one state over another.

You get: Equal opportunity for the commerce of all parts of the country.

ARTICLE 1
SECTION 9
CLAUSE 7

"No money shall be drawn from the Treasury, but in consequence of appropriations made by law; and a regular statement and account of the receipts and expenditures of all public money shall be published from time to time."

CLAUSE 8

"No title of nobility shall be granted by the United States; and no person holding any office of profit or trust under them shall, without the consent of the Congress, accept of any present, emolument, office, or title, of any kind whatever, from any king, prince, or foreign state."

You deny: To everyone in the government the right to spend money which has not been authorized by a law.

You get: (*a*) Assurance that your tax money is being spent only for authorized purposes; (*b*) an opportunity from time to time to see how your money is being spent.

ARTICLE 1
SECTION 10
CLAUSE 1

"No state shall enter into any treaty, alliance, or confederation; grant letters of marque and reprisal; coin money; emit bills of credit; make anything but gold and silver coin a tender in payment of debts; pass any bill of attainder, ex post facto law, or law impairing the obligation of contracts, or grant any title of nobility."

"You states must all keep an eye on this clause! It forbids you to do certain things which the federal government can do better. And it forbids you to do certain things which the people don't intend to have anybody do!"

You deny: To the states any powers to do certain things which you have already told the federal government it can or cannot do.

You get: Assurances (*a*) that no state will interfere with certain duties which are better handled by the federal government; (*b*) that no state will assume certain powers that you do not intend to grant to anyone.

ARTICLE 1
Section 10
Clause 2

"No state shall, without the consent of the Congress, lay any imposts or duties on imports or exports, except what may be absolutely necessary for executing its inspection laws; and the net produce of all duties and imposts, laid by any state on imports or exports, shall be for the use of the Treasury of the United States; and all such laws shall be subject to the revision and control of the Congress."

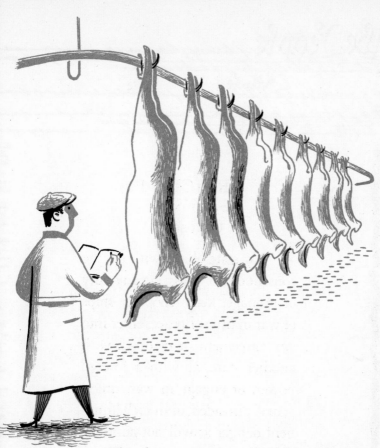

This clause prevents states with busy harbors, like New York or California, from charging duties on the foreign commerce of other states. But states may charge small fees to inspect interstate shipments of food or other products that might be harmful to health or morals.

You deny: To the state any right to tax goods moving across its borders except as needed to pay normal costs of inspection.

You get: A flow of commerce that is unrestricted, except by the uniform tariffs of the federal government.

ARTICLE 1
SECTION 10
CLAUSE 3

"No state shall, without the consent of Congress, lay any duty of tonnage, keep troops or ships of war in time of peace, enter into any agreement or compact with another state, or with a foreign power, or engage in war, unless actually invaded, or in such imminent danger as will not admit of delay."

"Duty of tonnage" is a tax laid on ships according to their own weight as they enter a port. States are forbidden to levy such taxes without the consent of Congress.

Agreements and compacts between states, with the consent of Congress, are not uncommon. For example, the Port of New York Authority, created by a compact between New York and New Jersey, built the George Washington Bridge and other facilities around New York Harbor. Such compacts are useful in handling local interstate problems.

ARTICLE
2

THE WHITE HOUSE

EXECUTIVE BRANCH

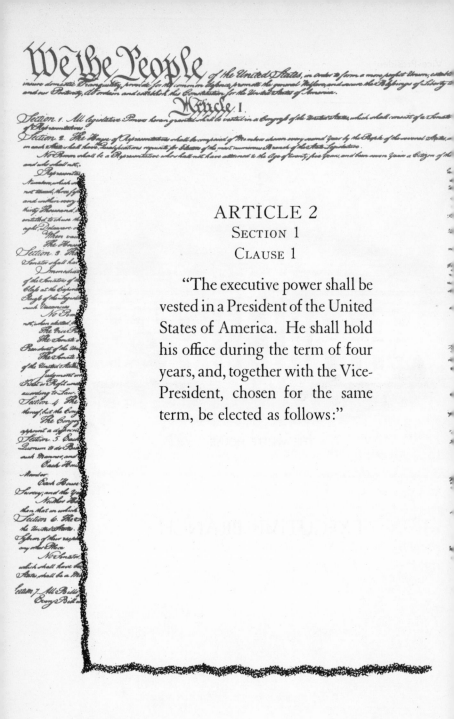

ARTICLE 2
SECTION 1
CLAUSE 1

"The executive power shall be vested in a President of the United States of America. He shall hold his office during the term of four years, and, together with the Vice-President, chosen for the same term, be elected as follows:"

Article 2 establishes the second great branch of our government. It is the executive branch, which carries out or enforces the laws that are passed by Congress. The Constitution assigns this authority and responsibility to the President. Thousands of people help him, but his job is still one of the hardest and most important in the world. In case he should die or for any other reason be unable to carry on, the Constitution provides for a Vice-President who can step into the President's job at a moment's notice.

You give: Full authority to the President of the United States to carry out all the executive duties of the country.

You get: A strong, centralized authority qualified to do what the laws of the nation require.

ARTICLE 2
SECTION 1
CLAUSE 2

"Each state shall appoint, in such manner as the Legislature thereof may direct, a number of electors, equal to the whole number of Senators and Representatives to which the state may be entitled in the Congress: but no Senator or Representative, or person holding an office of trust or profit under the United States, shall be appointed an elector."

CLAUSE 3

"The electors shall meet in their respective states and vote by ballot for two persons, of whom one at least shall not be an inhabitant of the same state with themselves. And they shall make a list of all the persons voted for, and of the number of votes for each, which list they shall sign and certify and transmit, sealed, to the seat of the government of the United States, directed to the president of the Senate. The president of the Senate shall, in the pres-

The Electoral College, as it is called, is made up of the electors chosen by each state to elect the President and Vice-President. It never meets as a group. Rather, the electors meet at their state capitols, vote, and send their choices to the president of the Senate.

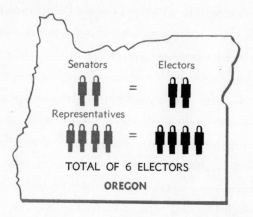

The makers of the Constitution thought it would be impractical, or even unwise, to elect a President and Vice-President by popular vote. Instead they outlined a plan under which, they thought, a special group of electors chosen by the state legislatures would decide who should hold these important offices. When the choices from all the states were tallied in Congress, the person with the highest number of votes would be President, while the runner-up would be Vice-President.

This plan did not work very well, and changes soon began to be made. Amendment 12 required electors to specify which of their choices they wanted for President and which for Vice-President (see page 222). In other re-

We the People of the United States, in order to form a more perfect Union, establish justice, insure domestic Tranquility, provide for the common defence, promote the general Welfare, and secure the Blessings of Liberty to ourselves and our Posterity, do ordain and establish this Constitution for the United States of America.

Article I.

Section 1. All legislative Powers herein granted shall be vested in a Congress of the United States, which shall consist of a Senate and House of Representatives.

Section 2. The House of Representatives shall be composed of Members chosen every second Year by the People of the several States, and the Electors in each State shall have the Qualifications requisite for Electors of the most numerous Branch of the State Legislature.

No Person shall be a Representative who shall not have attained to the Age of twenty five Years, and been seven Years a Citizen of the United States, and who shall not, when elected, be an Inhabitant of that State in which he shall be chosen.

-ence of the Senate and the House of Representatives, open all the certificates, and the votes shall then be counted. The person having the greatest number of votes shall be the President, if such number be a majority of the whole number of electors appointed; and if there be more than one who have such majority, and have an equal number of votes, then the House of Representatives shall immediately choose by ballot one of them for President; and if no person have a majority, then from the five highest on the list the said House shall in like manner choose the President. But in choosing the President, the vote shall be taken by states, the representation from each state having one vote. A quorum for this purpose shall consist of a member or members from two-thirds of the states, and a majority of all the states shall be necessary to a choice. In every case, after the choice of the President, the person having the greatest number of votes of the electors shall be the Vice President. But if there should remain two or more who have equal votes, the Senate shall choose from them by ballot the Vice-President."

spects, Amendment 12 left the plan about as it had been. But meantime an even more important change was beginning to be made, a change not recorded in our Constitution but one which custom has made a part of what is sometimes called our "Unwritten Constitution." That change has to do with the development of political parties.

The men who wrote the Constitution intended that groups of thoughtful men in the states would elect the President and Vice-President. Instead a group of powerful men in the Congress, called a caucus, decided whom they wanted to lead the nation and tried to force their choices on the nation. To combat this undemocratic trend, men with similar political views from all over the nation banded together to choose candidates whom the electors would be pledged to vote for. From those simple beginnings have grown the great political parties and the presidential elections that we know today.

At conventions held every four years each party selects its candidates for President and Vice-President (see page 247). In elections which follow the conventions, electors are chosen by each party in each of the states to cast its votes in the Electoral College. You actually vote for these electors, not for the candidates. But no elector ever goes back on his pledge to vote for his party's candidates, so that you do vote, in effect, for the candidates themselves. Thus, a custom has developed which provides for the popular election of the President and Vice-President.

ARTICLE 2
Section 1
Clause 4

"The Congress may determine the time of choosing the electors and the day on which they shall give their votes, which day shall be the same throughout the United States."

Clause 5

"No person except a natural-born citizen, ~~or a citizen of the United States at the time of the adoption of this Constitution,~~ shall be eligible to the office of President; neither shall any person be eligible to that office who shall not have attained to the age of thirty-five years and been fourteen years a resident within the United States."

QUALIFICATIONS FOR PRESIDENT

1. Natural-born citizen of the United States.
2. Age—not less than thirty-five years.
3. Fourteen years a resident of the United States.

ARTICLE 2
SECTION 1
CLAUSE 6

"In case of the removal of the President from office, or of his death, resignation, or inability to discharge the powers and duties of the said office, the same shall devolve on the Vice-President, and the Congress may by law provide for the case of removal, death, resignation, or inability, both of the President and Vice-President, declaring what officer shall then act as President, and such officer shall act accordingly until the disability be removed or a President shall be elected."

When President Franklin D. Roosevelt died in 1945 at a time of national crisis and was succeeded by Vice-President Harry Truman, people became concerned over what might happen if both President and Vice-President should die. Congress had passed a law in 1886 which stated that in this event the presidency should go to the Secretary of State and then in order through the other members of the President's Cabinet. But this would have meant that the highest elective office in the land would go to a person not elected by the people but rather appointed by the President. In 1947, therefore, Congress changed the Law of Presidential Succession to read that the Vice-President should be succeeded by the Speaker of the House of Representatives and then the President pro tempore of the Senate, both elected officers of the government. In the unlikely event that all four elected officers were not available, then the Cabinet officers would fall in line for the presidency.

ARTICLE 2
Section 1
Clause 7

"The President shall, at stated times, receive for his services a compensation, which shall neither be increased nor diminished during the period for which he shall have been elected, and he shall not receive within that period any other emolument from the United States, or any of them."

You give: Salary and expenses to the President, and also to the Vice-President, although the Constitution does not mention payment for the latter.

You get: Freedom from Congressional influence, since no President can have his salary raised or reduced during his term.

ARTICLE 2
SECTION 1
CLAUSE 8

"Before he enter on the execution of his office he shall take the following oath or affirmation: 'I do solemnly swear (or affirm) that I will faithfully execute the office of President of the United States, and will to the best of my ability, preserve, protect, and defend the Constitution of the United States.'"

An incoming President actually becomes the
new President at the moment the oath of office
is taken. By custom the oath is administered by
the Chief Justice of the Supreme Court on Inauguration Day in Washington, D.C.

ARTICLE 2
SECTION 2
CLAUSE 1

"The President shall be commander in chief of the Army and Navy of the United States, and of the militia of the several states when called into the actual service of the United States; he may require the opinion, in writing, of the principal officer in each of the executive departments, upon any subject relating to the duties of their respective offices, and he shall have power to grant reprieves and pardons for offenses against the United States, except in cases of impeachment."

The office of the President of the United States is one of the most powerful positions in the world. The Constitution devotes only 320 words to its duties and powers (not counting the statement of the veto power), but those few words, in Sections 2 and 3 of Article 2, cover a wide range of authority.

Commander in Chief
OF
The Armed Forces
AND OF
The Militia
OF THE SEVERAL STATES
WHEN IN SERVICE OF
THE UNITED STATES

The makers of the Constitution had several important points in mind when they assigned to the President the duties of the commander in chief of the armed forces. Among them were these: (1) they provided that the head of the armed forces should be elected by the people; (2) they prevented some nonelected head of the armed forces from seizing civil power and making himself President; (3) they prevented any President from becoming a dictator, since he can be head of the armed forces only so long as he is President, and a President can be impeached or voted out of office; (4) they placed in the hands of one man the immense civil and military powers that must be efficiently used in time of war.

"MAY GRANT REPRIEVES OR PARDONS FOR OFFENSES AGAINST THE UNITED STATES EXCEPT IN CASES OF IMPEACHMENT"

PARDONS AND REPRIEVES

LAW ENFORCEMENT

COMMANDER IN CHIEF

APPOINTMENTS

HEAD OF CABINET

TREATIES

EXECUTIVE POWERS OF THE PRESIDENT

The words "principal officer in each of the executive departments" imply that there will be various administrative departments to help the President carry out his duties. The heads of these departments have come to be known as the President's Cabinet.

You give: Authority to your President (*a*) to be head of all military forces; (*b*) to get advice from his Cabinet; (*c*) to pardon offenses against the United States when he deems it wise.

You get: (*a*) Civilian control of the armed forces; (*b*) administration of executive departments by officers responsible to the President; (*c*) a "last chance" for one who has been convicted of federal offenses.

ARTICLE 2
SECTION 2
CLAUSE 2

"He shall have power, by and with the advice and consent of the Senate, to make treaties, provided two-thirds of the Senators present concur; and he shall nominate and, by and with the advice and consent of the Senate, shall appoint ambassadors, other public ministers and consuls, judges of the Supreme Court, and all other officers of the United States, whose appointments are not herein provided for, and which shall be established by law; but the Congress may by law vest the appointment of such inferior officers, as they think proper, in the President alone, in the courts of law, or in the heads of departments."

CLAUSE 3

"The President shall have power to fill up all vacancies that may happen during the recess of the Senate, by granting commissions which shall expire at the end of their next session."

A treaty is an agreement between two or
more countries. Usually our State Department
handles the details. When details are complete,
the President must submit the treaty to the
Senate for approval by a two-thirds vote. The
Senate is a check on the President to insure
that he will make no agreements with other
nations which the representatives of the people
do not approve.

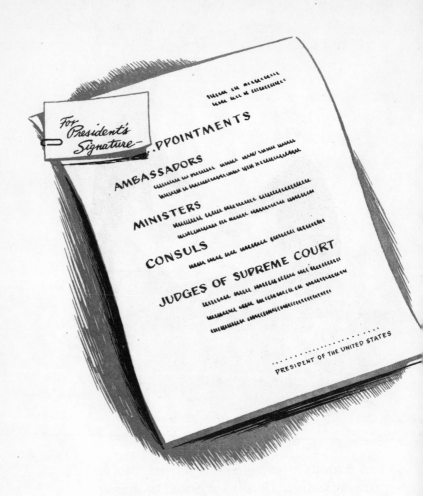

The Constitution makes a distinction between (1) officers so important that their appointment by the President should be made with the advice and consent of the Senate, and (2) "inferior officers" whose appointment can be entrusted to the President, to his Cabinet officers, or to judges without investigation by the Senate. The so-called inferior officers are not necessarily unimportant.

Among the important officials whose appointment the Senate must confirm, in addition to those mentioned in the Constitution, are these: officers of the armed forces, leading postmasters, customs officials, and members of important agencies such as the Atomic Energy Commission, the Federal Reserve Board, and the Interstate Commerce Commission. Congress itself may not make appointments.

If any government office falls vacant when Congress is not in session, the President may appoint someone to fill the post. Such appointments are known as *ad interim*, or "for the interval," appointments. At the next session of Congress the Senate may approve or disapprove the appointment.

Only a small percentage of the people who work for the government ever come to the attention of the Senate, the President, judges, or Cabinet officers. The responsibility for finding suitable people for most of these posts has been assigned to the Civil Service Commission. The commission conducts competitive examinations all over the country, for all kinds of jobs—from stenographers and laboratory technicians to forest rangers and airplane pilots. When job openings occur, they are offered to the people in each job category who have the highest scores in the civil service examinations. Thus, the government tries to find and keep the most competent people for these jobs, without regard to their political connections.

Government employees have not always been selected so carefully. Early Presidents were often obliged for political reasons to fire large numbers of employees so that their jobs could be filled by faithful party workers, who might be competent but often were not. This was called the "Spoils System," from an old sentence which says: "To the victor belong the spoils"—that is, the rewards of victory belong to the people who win. That system was inefficient and often unfair. Nearly all government employees can now be quite certain that they will keep their jobs, no matter who becomes President, provided they do what their jobs require of them.

You give: To the President authority (*a*) to make treaties with other countries, provided two-thirds of the Senate agrees to them; (*b*) to appoint many officials of the government, some with and some without consent of the Senate.

You get: (*a*) The most careful thought of both the President and the Senate in our all-important foreign relations; (*b*) careful selection of candidates for important government offices.

ARTICLE 2
Section 3

"He shall from time to time give to the Congress information of the state of the Union, and recommend to their consideration such measures as he shall judge necessary and expedient; he may, on extraordinary occasions, convene both houses, or either of them, and in case of disagreement between them, with respect to the time of adjournment, he may adjourn them to such time as he shall think proper; he shall receive ambassadors and other public ministers; he shall take care that the laws be faithfully executed, and shall commission all the officers of the United States."

THE DUTIES OF THE PRESIDENT

The President of the United States is required
by the Constitution to carry out certain duties.

DUTY 1—"STATE OF THE UNION" MESSAGE

DUTY 2—HE SHALL RECEIVE AMBASSADORS AND MINISTERS

DUTY 3—HE SHALL SEE THAT ALL LAWS ARE EXECUTED

DUTY 4—HE SHALL COMMISSION ALL OFFICERS OF THE UNITED STATES

Among his duties, the President is required to give information and make recommendations to Congress. The President is better able than anyone else to know the "state of the Union" and its needs from day to day, because hundreds of thousands of government employees throughout the country and around the world report back to their head offices, which in turn report to the President. His messages, now broadcast, are powerful political weapons, as is his power to call special sessions of Congress.

Among the most important duties of the President is "to take care that the laws be faithfully executed." He cannot do this personally. There are dozens of agencies in the Executive Department to help him enforce the laws.

You give: To the President (*a*) responsibility for informing Congress on the nation's affairs, with recommendations for improvements; (*b*) the right to call special sessions of Congress when necessary; (*c*) the right to receive the important representatives of foreign powers which have been officially recognized by the United States; (*d*) the immense responsibility of enforcing the federal laws; (*e*) the duty of signing all documents appointing officials to office.

You get: (*a*) Occasional bird's-eye views of national affairs; (*b*) assurance that Congress will be on the job when needed; (*c*) official examination of the credentials and intentions of foreign representatives; (*d*) assurance that the laws of Congress will be enforced; (*e*) a final scrutiny by the President of all important appointments.

ARTICLE 2
SECTION 4

"The President, Vice-President, and all civil officers of the United States shall be removed from office on impeachment for, and conviction of, treason, bribery, or other high crimes and misdemeanors."

Treason is committed when an officer of the government makes war against the United States or assists her enemies. Bribery means to accept or offer money or something else valuable in order to influence the affairs of government illegally. Other high crimes and misdemeanors include any misdoing for which the government has specified punishments. It may also mean any other action committed by an official which shows that he is morally unfit to hold office.

Methods of impeachment are explained on pages 26 and 39.

ARTICLE
3

THE SUPREME COURT

JUDICIAL BRANCH

ARTICLE 3
SECTION 1

"The judicial power of the United States shall be vested in one Supreme Court, and in such inferior courts as the Congress may from time to time ordain and establish. The judges, both of the Supreme and inferior courts, shall hold their offices during good behavior, and shall, at stated times, receive for their services a compensation, which shall not be diminished during their continuance in office."

The Supreme Court is the third branch of the United States government. Congress makes the laws, subject to the President's approval or veto; the President carries out and enforces the laws; the Supreme Court, called the judicial branch, interprets the laws. This includes the power to decide whether or not a law, either state or federal, is in accord with the Constitution. That immense power of the Supreme Court to declare laws "unconstitutional" is not definitely stated in the Constitution, but the Court has assumed it for more than a hundred years. It is an important safeguard in keeping our government within the powers and functions we have assigned to it.

The "inferior courts" authorized by Congress are shown on page 83.

You give (*a*) Authority to a system of federal courts to judge whether or not a law has been violated; (*b*) lasting jobs at good salaries to federal judges, provided they do nothing for which they may be impeached.

You get: (*a*) Uniform administration of justice; (*b*) review of federal and state laws in the light of the Constitution; (*c*) experienced judges, not elected by the voters and therefore not subject to the ups and downs of politics; (*d*) a judicial branch independent of Congress and President.

ARTICLE 3
SECTION 2
CLAUSE 1

"The judicial power shall extend to all cases, in law and equity, arising under this Constitution, the laws of the United States, and treaties made, or which shall be made, under their authority; to all cases affecting ambassadors, other public ministers and consuls; to all cases of admiralty and maritime jurisdiction; to controversies to which the United States shall be a party; to controversies between two or more states, ~~between a state and citizens of another state,~~ between citizens of different states; between citizens of the same state claiming lands under grants of different states, and between a state, or the citizens thereof, and foreign states, citizens, or subjects."*

* The Eleventh Amendment, adopted in 1798, changed this clause slightly. When a citizen of another state or of a foreign nation wishes to sue a state, he must sue in the courts of that state under its own laws and with its consent.

Lawyers make a distinction between "cases in law," which are related to the old English common law, and "cases in equity," which are related to another kind of legal procedure that grew up in England when the common law became too strict. The distinction is not often important to the average citizen.

Most of the cases which are tried in federal courts may be broken into two general classes, as shown below:

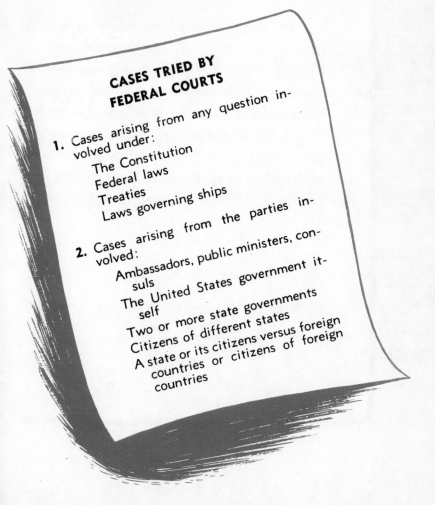

CASES TRIED BY FEDERAL COURTS

1. Cases arising from any question involved under:
   The Constitution
   Federal laws
   Treaties
   Laws governing ships

2. Cases arising from the parties involved:
   Ambassadors, public ministers, consuls
   The United States government itself
   Two or more state governments
   Citizens of different states
   A state or its citizens versus foreign countries or citizens of foreign countries

ARTICLE 3
SECTION 2
CLAUSE 2

"In all cases affecting ambassadors, other public ministers and consuls, and those in which a state shall be party, the Supreme Court shall have original jurisdiction. In all the other cases before mentioned, the Supreme Court shall have appellate jurisdiction, both as to law and fact, with such exceptions and under such regulations as the Congress shall make."

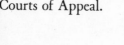

Certain cases, such as those involving states or official representatives of foreign nations, begin and end in the Supreme Court. This is called "original jurisdiction."

Most other federal cases begin and end in the district courts, of which there is at least one in each state. But the Supreme Court has the right to review the records of all such cases and to reverse the decisions of the lower courts if they are in error. Some cases may also be appealed to the Supreme Court from state courts. This right of the Supreme Court to review decisions of other courts is called "appellate jurisdiction." Usually the Court does not review a case unless it is appealed. The heavy responsibility of the Supreme Court in handling its appellate jurisdiction is shared in part by the United States Courts of Appeal.

ARTICLE 3
SECTION 2
CLAUSE 3

"The trial of all crimes, except in cases of impeachment, shall be by jury; and such trial shall be held in the state where the said crimes shall have been committed; but when not committed within any state, the trial shall be at such place or places as the Congress may by law have directed."*

* The provisions of this clause were expanded by Amendments 5, 6, and 7 (pages 204–9).

Crime, in the meaning of the Constitution, does not include certain petty offenses. But it does include all other criminal offenses, which must be tried before a jury. This is a very important safeguard for your life and liberty.

You give: Instructions (*a*) that your guilt or innocence may be determined only by twelve fellow citizens; (*b*) that you must be tried in the state where your crime is said to have been committed.

You get: Protection from arbitrary decisions of courts and judges to imprison or fine you. The function of the jury is to decide the facts. Before you can be held guilty, all the jurors must agree.

ARTICLE 3
SECTION 3
CLAUSE 1

"Treason against the United States shall consist only in levying war against them, or in adhering to their enemies, giving them aid and comfort. No person shall be convicted of treason unless on the testimony of two witnesses to the same overt act, or on confession in open court."

Kings of England had called many acts "treason," among them merely criticizing the king. To prevent such tyranny, the Constitution clearly defines what it means by "treason," and under what conditions a person may be convicted of it.

You give: (*a*) A strict definition of what is meant by treason; (*b*) instructions which prevent its misuse.

You get: Protection (*a*) for your government against a very serious crime; (*b*) for yourself against vague or "trumped-up" charges of treason.

ARTICLE 3
SECTION 3
CLAUSE 2

"The Congress shall have power to declare the punishment of treason, but no attainder of treason shall work corruption of blood or forfeiture except during the life of the person attainted."

The punishment set forth by Congress for treason is death, or not less than five years in prison and a $10,000 fine.

English rulers had sometimes gone so far as to deprive the descendants of traitors of their civil liberties and their property. The second part of this clause forbids this injustice against innocent people.

You give: To Congress the power to set the punishment which the courts may impose for treason, but you limit punishment to the life of the traitor.

You get: (*a*) A guaranty of severe punishments for one of the worst crimes that anyone can commit; (*b*) protection for innocent people.

ARTICLE
4

CONCERNING THE STATES

ARTICLE 4
SECTION 1

"Full faith and credit shall be given in each state to the public acts, records, and judicial proceedings of every other state. And the Congress may by general laws prescribe the manner in which such acts, records, and proceedings shall be proved, and the effect thereof."

There would be endless confusion in the country if the laws, the birth and death certificates, and the court decisions of one state were not honored in the other states. This clause provides that they will be honored, according to regulations passed by Congress. Thus, if a court in your state orders your neighbor to pay you some money, your neighbor cannot avoid payment simply by moving to another state. Courts in that state will honor your right to the money as though they had granted it themselves.

You give: Instructions that each state shall recognize the legal actions of every other state.

You get: Recognition in every state of your legal rights at home.

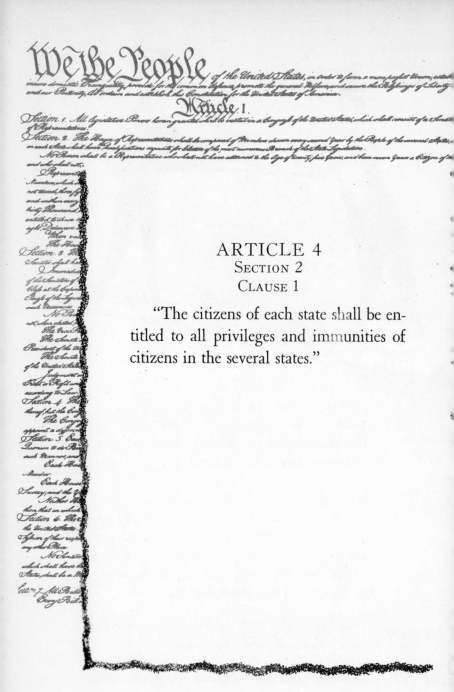

ARTICLE 4
SECTION 2
CLAUSE 1

"The citizens of each state shall be entitled to all privileges and immunities of citizens in the several states."

This clause makes it possible for the average American to feel that he is a member of a great nation as well as of his own state. It means that you may go freely from one state to another and be treated about the same way as everyone else. You may move, go into business, buy or sell property, get married, and pay taxes under the same rules and regulations as all other citizens of the state in which you find yourself. Only a few special privileges, such as voting, may be withheld until you become a citizen of that state.

You give: Instructions that the states must offer fair treatment to the citizens of other states.

You get: (*a*) Protection against unfairness as you go from one state to another; (*b*) membership in a great nation as well as in your own state.

ARTICLE 4
SECTION 2
CLAUSE 2

"A person charged in any state with treason, felony, or other crime, who shall flee from justice, and be found in another state, shall, on demand of the executive authority of the state from which he fled, be delivered up, to be removed to the state having jurisdiction of the crime."

Governor

Criminal

Governor

STATE LINE

Each state must arrest, try, and punish those who break its laws. So that criminals may not escape punishment by running off to another state, this clause provides legal means to return them to the states where their crimes were committed. The process is called "extradition."

The clause states that the executive authority, that is, the Governor, "shall" return the criminal to the state where he committed his crime. "Shall," however, has been interpreted to mean "may." In other words, a Governor cannot be forced to turn over a criminal if he sees good reason not to. In practice, however, a captured criminal is nearly always returned for trial.

You give: Instructions for dealing with fugitive criminals.

You get: Assurance that criminals cannot evade state laws by fleeing to another state.

ARTICLE 4
SECTION 2
CLAUSE 3

~~"No person held to service or labor in one state, under the laws thereof, escaping into another, shall, in consequence of any law or regulation therein, be discharged from such service or labor, but shall be delivered up on claim of the party to whom such service or labor may be due."~~*

* This clause referred to runaway slaves. Amendment 13 made it meaningless. (See page 226.)

SECTION 3
CLAUSE 1

"New states may be admitted by the Congress into this Union; but no new state shall be formed or erected within the jurisdiction of any other state, nor any state be formed by the junction of two or more states, or parts of states, without the consent of the Legislatures of the states concerned as well as of the Congress."

Under this clause, Congress admitted to the Union all of the states except the original thirteen.

If the people of California wanted to split their state into two states, they could do so provided they had the consent of Congress and of the California Legislature. Or, if the people of southern California wanted to unite with a section of Arizona to form a new state, they would need the consent of the Legislatures of California and Arizona, as well as of Congress.

You give: To Congress the authority to admit new states to the Union, but you require the consent of state Legislatures if state areas are involved.

You get: (*a*) A means by which the nation may expand; (*b*) protection from groups which might try to break up states into smaller units to gain local or national power.

ARTICLE 4
SECTION 3
CLAUSE 2

"The Congress shall have power to dispose of and make all needful rules and regulations respecting the territory or other property belonging to the United States; and nothing in this Constitution shall be so construed as to prejudice any claims of the United States, or of any particular state."

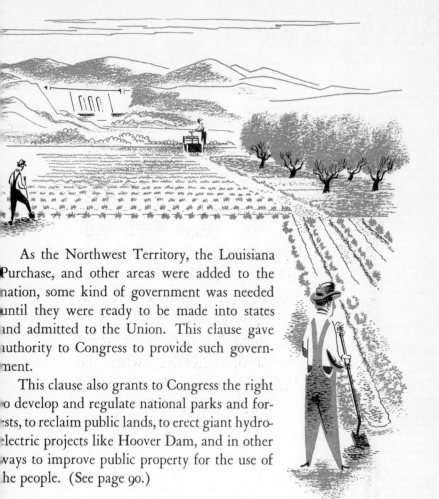

As the Northwest Territory, the Louisiana Purchase, and other areas were added to the nation, some kind of government was needed until they were ready to be made into states and admitted to the Union. This clause gave authority to Congress to provide such government.

This clause also grants to Congress the right to develop and regulate national parks and forests, to reclaim public lands, to erect giant hydroelectric projects like Hoover Dam, and in other ways to improve public property for the use of the people. (See page 90.)

You give: To Congress authority to govern the territories and regulate the use of other property of the United States government.

You get: (*a*) Government for territories; (*b*) protection of public property through the supervision of your elected representatives; (*c*) improvement of parks, forests, deserts, and other property for the use of all the people.

ARTICLE 4
Section 4

"The United States shall guarantee to every state in this Union a republican form of government, and shall protect each of them against invasion; and, on application of the Legislature, or of the executive (when the Legislature cannot be convened), against domestic violence."

The United States government guarantees to each of the states:

1. A "republican" form of government.
2. Protection against invasion.
3. Protection, when needed, against riots or other disturbances within the state.

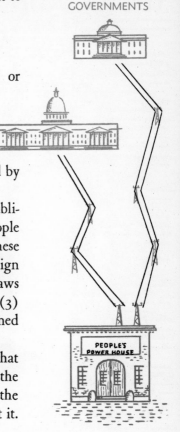

STATE GOVERNMENTS

FEDERAL GOVERNMENT

PEOPLE'S POWER HOUSE

This clause outlines the obligations owed by the federal government to the states.

The Constitution does not define "a republican form of government," but most people would agree that such a government has these characteristics, at least: (1) that the sovereign power belongs to the people; (2) that all laws are made by representatives of the people; (3) that the powers of the government are defined and limited by a written constitution.

If any state should adopt a government that violated such principles as these, it would be the responsibility of Congress, or perhaps of the President, to step in and do something about it.

You give: An obligation to your federal government in certain extreme cases to protect the political rights, the property, and the lives of the people in all the states.

You get: (a) Assurance that your state will not be turned into a dictatorship; (b) the whole force of the United States government to protect your state against invasion; (c) the help of the federal government if your state is unable to handle riots or other local crises.

ARTICLE
5

HOW AMENDMENTS

ARE MADE

ARTICLE 5

"The Congress, whenever two-thirds of both houses shall deem it necessary, shall propose amendments to this Constitution, or, on the application of the Legislatures of two-thirds of the several states, shall call a convention for proposing amendments, which, in either case, shall be valid to all intents and purposes, as part of this Constitution, when ratified by the Legislatures of three-fourths of the several states, or by conventions in three-fourths thereof, as the one or the other mode of ratification may be proposed by the Congress, provided that ~~no amendment which may be made prior to the year one thousand eight hundred and eight shall in any manner affect the first and fourth clauses in the Ninth Section of the First Article, and that~~ no state, without its consent, shall be deprived of its equal suffrage in the Senate."

All through the long, hot summer of 1787, the delegates to the Constitutional Convention labored to complete the plans for your House of Freedom. As their difficult work drew to a close, they felt that they had planned a structure in which the citizens of the United States could live in peace and harmony, each enjoying his own rights while also respecting the rights of others.

But the wise men who drafted the Constitution could not be sure that they had thought of everything. They realized that generations of citizens not yet born would face problems quite different from those of the new nation. So, while remaining convinced of the basic soundness of their plan, they made provision in Article 5 for alterations to be made from time to time. Alterations of this kind are called amendments. The next few pages explain how the Constitution may be amended.

There are two main steps that must be taken to amend the Constitution. These are, first, the proposal of the amendment and, second, approval by the states.

Amendments may be proposed in two ways: (1) by a two-thirds vote in both the Senate and the House of Representatives; (2) in a national convention called by Congress when asked to do so by the Legislatures of two-thirds of the states.

Approval of the states to an amendment, called ratification, may also be obtained in two ways: (1) by the Legislatures of the states; (2) by special conventions called in the states. Congress decides which method of ratification shall be used. If three-fourths of the states approve

AMENDMENTS ARE PROPOSED
BY

TWO-THIRDS OF EACH
HOUSE OF CONGRESS

OR

NATIONAL CONVENTIONS
CALLED BY CONGRESS

the amendment, by either method, it becomes law for all the states as part of the Constitution.

So far all twenty-one amendments have been proposed in Congress, and it is unlikely that one will ever be proposed by a national convention. By the time popular desire for an amendment had reached the point where two-thirds of the state Legislatures asked for a convention, Congress would already have proposed the amendment to save time, expense, and trouble.

All amendments except Amendment 21 were ratified by state Legislatures. Ratification by special conventions in the states provides a more direct expression of the feelings of the people about an amendment, but costs more in money, time, and effort.

AMENDMENTS ARE RATIFIED BY

> **LEGISLATURES OF THREE-FOURTHS OF THE STATES**

OR

> **CONVENTIONS IN THREE-FOURTHS OF THE STATES**

YOUR HOUSE OF FREEDOM

THE AMENDING PROCESS PREVENTS THIS!

Article 5, by which the Constitution provides for its own amendment, is one of the most important ideas included in our form of government. When enough of the people in the nation want to make a change in the government, they may do so in an orderly way. They may vote for representatives, both in Congress and in their state Legislatures, who will carry out the change.

In the United States it is not necessary for the people to use revolution and bloodshed to change the government. You may sometimes hear of groups of people "going underground," and "plotting to overthrow the government of the United States." You are entitled to be suspicious of such groups. For some reason they are unwilling to follow the process of orderly change which is outlined in the Constitution. Instead, they work secretly to attain their own selfish aims.

The methods by which the Constitution may be amended are not easy to apply. Some people think the process should be made easier, but the men who planned your House of Freedom had sound reasons in mind when they made it difficult. Calling upon their knowledge and their practical experience in government, they wrote what they hoped was a sound and lasting Constitution. Knowing that future conditions and future needs might be different, however, they wanted the people of the United States to be able to alter the plans from time to time—but only after an extraordinary majority of the people had agreed that the changes were necessary.

Many amendments have been suggested and discussed. But only twenty-seven have been proposed and only twenty-one adopted. That stability reflects another point of wisdom that was shown by the men who wrote the Constitution. They concerned themselves with basic matters, leaving details to be worked out by interpretation and experience. If hundreds of basic changes had been made in the plans, our House of Freedom might have become an architectural monstrosity.

Thanks to the difficult procedures required for changing the Constitution, frivolous and dangerous amendments are avoided. Congress must think out a change carefully before proposing it. The people of the states consider each proposal, debate it on street corners, in their newspapers, and over the radio. Finally, their elected representatives bring their opinions to a vote, either for approval or disapproval.

By such means as these, our House of Freedom has kept its basic structure for over a hundred years and still has been kept up to date. Roof pitches have been altered, a wing or two has been added, new windows and doors give better ventilation, modern lighting and plumbing are installed. Thus, each new generation of citizens has a modern house to live in, but one whose basic plans have stood the test of time.

Article 5 concludes, "that no state, without its consent, shall be deprived of its equal suffrage in the Senate." Article 1, Section 3, provides that each state, regardless of size, shall elect two Senators to Congress. The small states had insisted on this provision, and here they insisted further that large states should not amend the Constitution to deprive them of that safeguard.

You give: Permission for the Constitution to be changed, but only through co-operation of federal and state governments.

You get: (*a*) A means by which amendments can be made when they become necessary or desirable; (*b*) assurance that the Constitution will be changed only when an extraordinary majority of the people desire it.

ARTICLE
6

THE SUPREME LAW
AND OTHER PROVISIONS

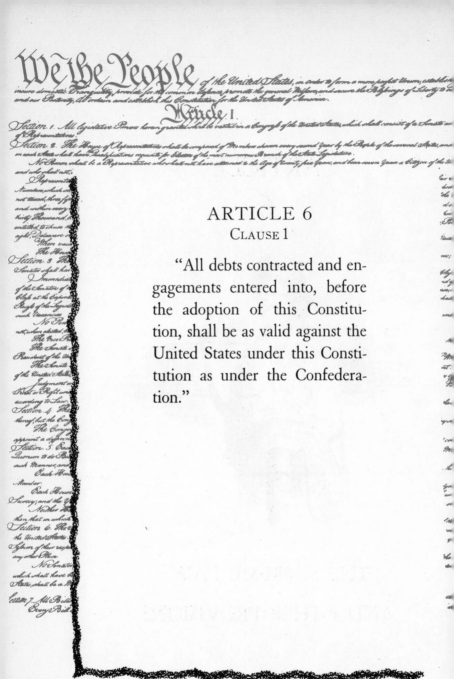

ARTICLE 6
Clause 1

"All debts contracted and engagements entered into, before the adoption of this Constitution, shall be as valid against the United States under this Constitution as under the Confederation."

When changes of government had occurred in other nations, the new government had sometimes refused to pay debts incurred by the old. This clause announced our intention to pay off the debts incurred under the Articles of Confederation.

When the new government began, the national debt was over $50,000,000. However, because of the insecurity of the new nation, the bonds representing this debt were actually worth only about one-fourth of that amount. Alexander Hamilton, first Secretary of the Treasury, convinced Congress not only to pay off the national debt at its face value, but also to pay the debts incurred by the states in their struggle for independence.

Thanks to the honest financial policy begun at that time and continued ever since, the United States government has always found it easy to borrow money at low rates of interest.

ARTICLE 6
Clause 2

"This Constitution and the laws of the United States which shall be made in pursuance thereof, and all treaties made, or which shall be made, under the authority of the United States, shall be the supreme law of the land, and the judges in every state shall be bound thereby, anything in the Constitution or laws of any state to the contrary notwithstanding."

So far as the Constitution is concerned, there are two levels of government—federal and state —to which the people have assigned certain powers. State governments, however, have assigned part of their powers to the local governments in counties, towns, and cities. Thus, in practice, we have three levels of government, each with certain powers.

When powers have been divided up in that way, there must be some system of priority to settle disputes as to which is superior. This clause specifies that the Constitution, the treaties, and the laws of the United States shall have priority over state and local laws whenever there is conflict between them. Without this provision, the authority of the federal government could be undermined by actions of the states.

ORDER OF LAWS IN UNITED STATES

1. The Constitution of the United States
2. Laws and treaties of the federal government
3. Constitutions of the states
4. Laws passed by the states
5. Laws passed by county, town, and city governments

You give: Orders that the Constitution, treaties, and laws of the United States shall be superior to state and local laws.

You get: A firm Union that cannot be easily destroyed by disputes over the relative powers of the states and the federal government.

ARTICLE 6
Clause 3

"The Senators and Representatives before mentioned, and the members of the several state Legislatures, and all executive and judicial officers, both of the United States and of the several states, shall be bound by oath or affirmation to support this Constitution; but no religious test shall ever be required as a qualification to any office or public trust under the United States."

"I do solemnly swear that I will support and defend the Constitution of the United States against all enemies, foreign or domestic; that I will bear true faith and allegiance to the same . . ."

Cabinet Member

To make doubly sure that federal and state officials of all kinds would know their obligation to uphold and defend the Constitution of the United States, this clause was inserted. Without loyalty to the Constitution and all that depends upon it, our liberties, privileges, and obligations would soon become impaired if not destroyed.

The men who wrote the Constitution believed that separation of religion and the government would help to avoid conflicts at home. The final words of this clause, therefore, prevent anyone from being disqualified from office in the federal government because of his religion.

You give: Instructions requiring every official of the federal and state governments to swear that he will uphold the Constitution.

You get: The solemn assurance of your government officials that they will be loyal to the trust you place in them.

ARTICLE
7

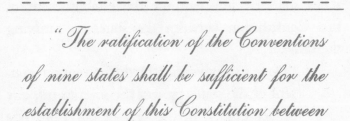

" *The ratification of the Conventions of nine states shall be sufficient for the establishment of this Constitution between the states so ratifying the same.*"

RATIFICATION
OF THE CONSTITUTION

ARTICLE 7

"The ratification of the Conventions of nine states shall be sufficient for the establishment of this Constitution between the states so ratifying the same.

"Done in Convention by the unanimous consent of the states present the seventeenth day of September, in the year of our Lord one thousand seven hundred and eighty-seven and of the Independence of the United States of America the twelfth. In witness whereof, we have hereunto subscribed our names.

GEORGE WASHINGTON, *President and Deputy from Virginia*

Attest: WILLIAM JACKSON, *Secretary**

---

* Rhode Island sent no delegate to the Constitutional Convention.

of the United States, in order to form a more perfect Union, establish Justice, insure domestic Tranquility, provide for the common defence, promote the general Welfare, and secure the Blessings of Liberty to ourselves and our Posterity, do ordain and establish this Constitution for the United States of America.

Article I

All legislative Powers herein granted shall be vested in a Congress of the United States, which shall consist of a Senate and House of Representatives.

The House of Representatives shall be composed of Members chosen every second Year by the People of the several States, and the Electors in each State shall have the Qualifications requisite for Electors of the most numerous Branch of the State Legislature.

No Person shall be a Representative who shall not have attained to the Age of twenty five Years, and been seven Years a Citizen of the United States, and who shall not,

NEW HAMPSHIRE
John Langdon
Nicholas Gilman

MASSACHUSETTS
Nathaniel Gorham
Rufus King

CONNECTICUT
William Samuel Johnson
Roger Sherman

NEW YORK
Alexander Hamilton

NEW JERSEY
William Livingston
David Brearley
William Paterson
Jonathan Dayton

PENNSYLVANIA
Benjamin Franklin
Thomas Mifflin
Robert Morris
George Clymer
Thomas Fitzsimons
Jared Ingersoll
James Wilson
Gouverneur Morris

DELAWARE
George Read
Gunning Bedford, Jr.
John Dickinson
Richard Bassett
Jacob Broom

MARYLAND
James McHenry
Dan of St. Thomas Jennifer
Daniel Carroll

VIRGINIA
John Blair
James Madison, Jr.

NORTH CAROLINA
William Blount
Richard Dobbs Spaight
Hugh Williamson

SOUTH CAROLINA
John Rutledge
Charles Cotesworth Pinckney
Pierce Butler

GEORGIA
William Few
Abraham Baldwin

DISCUSSION OF CONSTITUTION

After the Constitution was signed by the delegates, it was submitted to the Congress. In the debate which followed, John Adams said, "Our people must be consulted, invited to erect the whole building with their own hands, upon the broadest foundations."

Late in September of 1787, Congress sent the Constitution to the states for ratification. Less than a year later, special conventions in eleven of the states had ratified the famous document, making it the supreme law of the land.

The actual building of the new government began in the spring of 1789, when George Washington was inaugurated the first President. Before summer of the following year, North Carolina and Rhode Island had ratified the Constitution. A firm Union of thirteen states was now pledged to support the Constitution and to build for all the citizens of the United States a new House of Freedom.

When the Constitution was being ratified, many people feared that the new government might abuse its powers. They insisted that the Constitution should contain more specific protection for the rights of the people. The First Congress, therefore, submitted twelve amendments to the states for ratification. Ten of these, called the Bill of Rights, were ratified in 1791. They apply only to the federal government. But all of the states have included similar bills of rights in their own constitutions.

ELECTION OF DELEGATES
TO STATE CONVENTION

STATE CONVENTION
ON RATIFICATION OF
THE CONSTITUTION

AMENDMENTS TO THE CONSTITUTION
I - IO

★ *The Bill of Rights* ★

Adopted in 1791

AMENDMENT 1

"Congress shall make no law respecting an establishment of religion, or prohibiting the free exercise thereof; or abridging the freedom of speech, or of the press; or the right of the people peaceably to assemble, and to petition the government for a redress of grievances."

Amendment 1 contains four important safeguards: (1) Congress may not create any official religion. Nor may it prevent you from worshiping as you see fit so long as you do not violate any laws nor infringe upon the rights of other people. (2) With few exceptions, you are free to say, write, or print anything you like. (3) Congress cannot prevent you from gathering together with other people to discuss anything you like, including alterations in the government. (4) You are free to go to your government and ask that abuses be corrected.

You deny: To Congress any power to interfere with your right to worship, to express yourself, to meet with other people, or to go to the government with your grievances.

You get: Protection against federal interference in four fundamental human rights. In many foreign countries, such rights as these are not protected by law.

AMENDMENT 2

"A well-regulated militia being necessary to the security of a free state, the right of the people to keep and bear arms shall not be infringed."

A large national army can become a threat to a free people, for its leaders may seize the government and deprive the people of their rights. Fearing such an army, early citizens of the United States chose to place their security very largely in the hands of state militia, or citizen armies. This amendment was added to keep the federal government from passing any rules that would interfere with the lawful possession and use of arms by the people.

You deny: To the federal government the power to interfere with your ownership and use of weapons for lawful purposes.

You get: Protection against abuse of power by a national army.

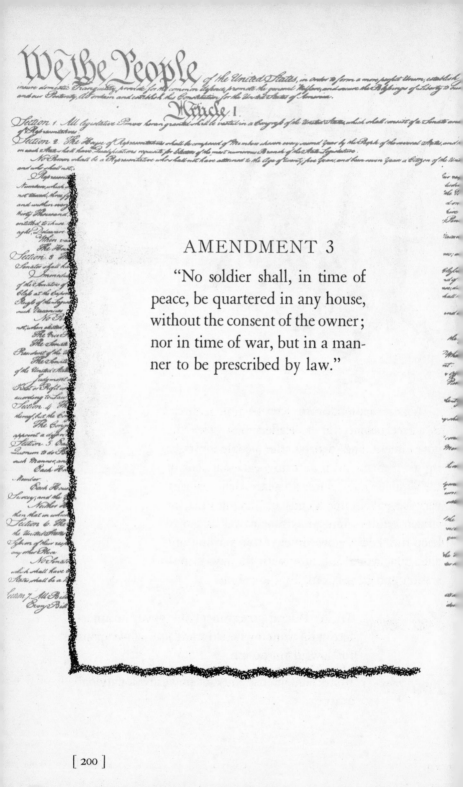

AMENDMENT 3

"No soldier shall, in time of peace, be quartered in any house, without the consent of the owner; nor in time of war, but in a manner to be prescribed by law."

Before the Revolution, American Colonists were often required by the British Government to take soldiers into their homes and give them food and lodging. The people bitterly resented this imposition on their homes, and were determined that their new government should never practice it, except under law in time of war.

You deny: To the federal government the right to quarter soldiers in your home except when clearly necessary.

You get: Protection against invasion of your property and privacy.

AMENDMENT 4

"The right of the people to be secure in their persons, houses, papers, and effects, against unreasonable searches and seizures, shall not be violated; and no warrants shall issue, but upon probable cause, supported by oath or affirmation, and particularly describing the place to be searched, and the persons or things to be seized."

British officers in America had often violated
an old English principle which held that officials of the government had no right to arrest
a person or to enter his home and search it without legal authority. The people added this
amendment to prevent such arrests and searches
without a warrant from a judge. A judge will
not issue a warrant until he is convinced that
there is good reason for the arrest or the search.
This is a safeguard not enjoyed by citizens of
many nations.

You deny: To federal officials the authority to arrest you
or to search your home or other possessions without a warrant.

You get: Protection of your liberty and privacy except
when it seems clear that you have broken the
law.

AMENDMENT 5

"No person shall be held to answer for a capital or other infamous crime unless on a presentment or indictment of a Grand Jury, except in cases arising in the land or naval forces, or in the militia, when in actual service, in time of war or public danger; nor shall any person be subject, for the same offense, to be twice put in jeopardy of life or limb; nor shall be compelled, in any criminal case, to be a witness against himself; nor be deprived of life, liberty, or property, without due process of law; nor shall private property be taken for public use, without just compensation."

"I must warn you! Anything you say may be used against you!"

The first half of this amendment means that the federal government cannot bring a person to trial for an important crime until a Grand Jury has weighed the charges against him and decided that they are probably true. (Capital crimes and infamous crimes include all crimes except minor ones, which are called misdemeanors.)

The rest of this amendment means: (1) that if you have been acquitted of a crime, you may not be tried again for the same crime; (2) that you cannot be compelled in a criminal case to say anything that would hurt your side of the case; (3) that the federal government may not execute or imprison you, or take away your property, except according to fair methods authorized by law; (4) that if the federal government needs your property for some good reason, you must be paid a fair price before you give it up.

You deny: To the government certain dictatorial powers over your life, your freedom, and your property.

You get: Safeguards that are vitally important to a free people.

AMENDMENT 6

"In all criminal prosecutions, the accused shall enjoy the right to a speedy and public trial, by an impartial jury of the state and district wherein the crime shall have been committed, which district shall have been previously ascertained by law, and to be informed of the nature and cause of the accusation; to be confronted with the witnesses against him; to have compulsory process for obtaining witnesses in his favor, and to have the assistance of counsel for his defense."

This amendment details certain rights which the federal government must extend to a person if he is arrested on a criminal charge. He is entitled to: (1) a public trial as soon as possible after his arrest; (2) a jury of twelve unbiased citizens living in the area where the crime is said to have been committed; (3) detailed information about the accusation, so that he may prepare his defense; (4) personal appearance in court, so that he may see and hear the witnesses who testify against him; (5) the help of the government, if necessary, in bringing favorable witnesses to court; (6) a lawyer to defend him, paid for by the government if the accused person is unable to pay him.

You give: Precise instructions to guarantee a fair trial for persons accused of crime.

You get: Protection against trials conducted according to any other methods, some of which might be unfair.

AMENDMENT 7

"In suits at common law, where the value in controversy shall exceed twenty dollars, the right of trial by jury shall be preserved, and no fact tried by a jury shall be otherwise re-examined in any court of the United States than according to the rules of the common law."

"My client demands a trial by jury!"

Amendments 5 and 6 refer to cases involving criminal laws. Amendment 7 refers to cases arising under the common law (see page 147). As used here, this means that a suit in the federal courts between two or more persons to settle their mutual rights and duties (usually called civil cases) must be tried by a jury. A jury is not necessary if less than $20 is involved or if both parties agree not to have one.

When a case has been appealed to a higher court, the appellate judge or judges may not question any establishment of fact in the jury's verdict. But the verdict may be changed (1) if the law was not correctly interpreted, or (2) if the evidence presented to the jury was not adequate to support the establishment of fact.

You give: Instructions (*a*) that provide for a jury trial in all civil cases except petty ones; (*b*) that tell the courts exactly how far they may go in questioning the work of the jury.

You get: (*a*) Protection against unfair decisions in civil cases; (*b*) respect for the verdict of the jury; (*c*) the possibility of a different decision if the jury fails in its duty.

AMENDMENT 8

"Excessive bail shall not be required, nor excessive fines imposed, nor cruel and unusual punishments inflicted."

After a person has been arrested and told what law he has broken, he is usually allowed to leave the jail until his trial, provided that either he or someone else puts up "bail." Bail is a certain amount of money, or a similar amount of property, that is placed in the hands of the court to guarantee that the accused person will appear when the trial is held. This amendment forbids federal judges to name unreasonable figures for bail. It also outlaws torture or unreasonable fines and imprisonment as punishment for crime.

You give: Instructions that provide fair treatment for persons accused, as well as convicted, of crimes.

You get: Protection against unreasonable treatment in the courts.

AMENDMENT 9

"The enumeration in the Constitution of certain rights shall not be construed to deny or disparage others retained by the people."

In the first eight amendments, certain rights belonging to the people are singled out and emphasized, so that the federal government will make no mistake about them. It was not possible, however, to list all of the rights which the people were keeping for themselves or assigning to the states. For that reason, Amendment 9 was added so that the federal government would not try to restrict fundamental rights simply because they were not mentioned in the Constitution. In practice it has been of no importance.

You deny: To the federal government any authority over certain unspecified and indefinite rights.

You get: (*a*) Protection against interference with any rights that were not thought of in 1791; (*b*) further assurance that the people's power will not be seized by a dictator.

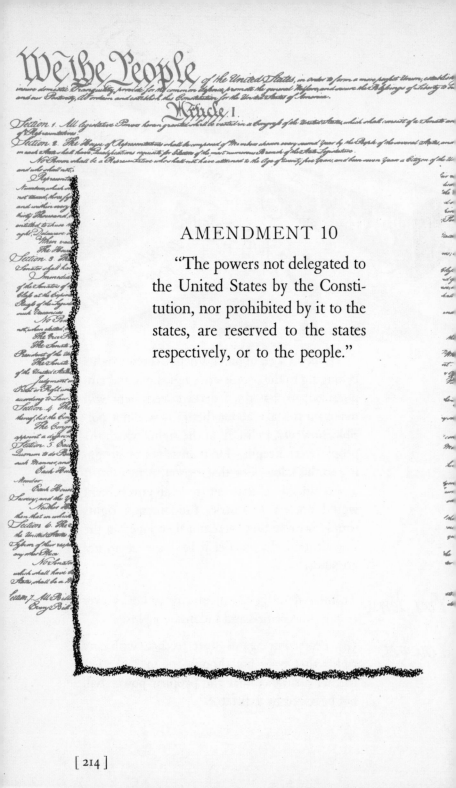

AMENDMENT 10

"The powers not delegated to the United States by the Constitution, nor prohibited by it to the states, are reserved to the states respectively, or to the people."

UNDELEGATED POWERS OF THE PEOPLE

THE CONSTITUTION OF THE UNITED STATES

TO THE STATES

TO THE UNITED STATES

THIS AMENDMENT IS OF GREAT IMPORTANCE TO <u>YOU</u>

"Powers not delegated . . . . are reserved
. . . . to the people." Those words are of great
importance. The Constitution of the United
States was the first written constitution based
on the belief that *all* political power always has
belonged to the people. John Adams said, "You
have rights antecedent to all earthly governments; rights that cannot be repealed or re-
strained by human laws; rights derived from the
Great Legislator of the Universe." That is what
those eight important words mean to you.

Each state had its own constitution which
assigned certain powers to the state government
and reserved others for the people. Under the
Articles of Confederation, the states had assigned a few of their powers to the national government. In this Constitution, the people were
assigning powers directly to the national government. Because of widespread fear that the

new government might try to employ powers that were not granted, this amendment was added. It makes clear that the federal government was to have only those powers assigned to it, and no more. Some other powers were left to the states. The remaining powers were kept by the people and were not to be used at all unless the people decided to assign them through an amendment to the Constitution.

State governments are concerned with such duties as education, improvement of roads, police forces, and public health and safety. Some of their powers in these matters are assigned to county, town, and city governments. As for the people of the states themselves, state constitutions contain "bills of rights" similar to those in the national Constitution. Thus, the people have told their state governments, as well as the federal government, just which powers they are delegating and which they are keeping in their own hands.

You give: Clear-cut orders to the federal government not to assume powers that have not been assigned to it.

You get: Added assurance that political power in your nation will be wielded only by those to whom you have assigned it.

Amendment 10 concludes the Bill of Rights, important safeguards enjoyed by all citizens of the United States and not enjoyed by millions of other people throughout the world. Their value to you is very great, and you should always be alert to protect them.

AMENDMENTS TO THE CONSTITUTION
11-21

★ *Additional*

Amendments ★

For dates of adoption,
see individual amendments

AMENDMENT 11
(*Adopted in 1798*)

"The judicial power of the United States shall not be construed to extend to any suit in law or equity, commenced or prosecuted against one of the United States, by citizens of another state, or by citizens or subjects of any foreign state."

State of Texas

"If you wish to sue the State of Texas, you'll have to sue in the courts of Texas. Uncle Sam can't help you!"

TEXAS

This amendment was added to clear up a misunderstanding that arose under Article 3, Section 2, Clause 1 (page 146). It was said there that federal courts could try cases involving controversies "between a state and citizens of another state." When ratifying the Constitution, the states took this to mean that they might bring citizens of other states into court, but that citizens of other states could not bring them into court without their consent. That distinction had been long established. When the Supreme Court ruled under Article 3 that a citizen of one state could sue another state, the states demanded this amendment.

You give: A clarification of the judicial power of the federal government.

You get: Protection for a traditional power of the states.

AMENDMENT 12
(*Adopted in 1804*)

"The electors shall meet in their respective states, and vote by ballot for President and Vice-President, one of whom, at least, shall not be an inhabitant of the same state with themselves; they shall name in their ballots the person voted for as President, and in distinct ballots the person voted for as Vice-President, and they shall make distinct lists of all persons voted for as President and of all persons voted for as Vice-President, and of the number of votes for each, which lists they shall sign and certify, and transmit, sealed, to the seat of the government of the United States, directed to the President of the Senate; the President of the Senate shall, in the presence of the Senate and House of Representatives, open all the certificates, and the votes shall then be counted. The person having the greatest number of votes for President shall be the President, if such number be a majority of the whole number of electors appointed; and if no person have such majority, then from the persons having the highest numbers, not exceeding three, on the list of those voted for as President, the House of

This amendment alters Article 2, Section 1, Clause 3 (page 114), by requiring that members of the Electoral College vote for a President and Vice-President on separate ballots. The amendment became necessary after the election of 1800. By that time political parties had begun to select candidates. All electors of the Democratic-Republican party voted for Thomas Jefferson and Aaron Burr, which made a tie vote when the ballots were counted. Most of these electors wanted Jefferson for President, Burr for Vice-President. But when the tie vote was sent to the House of Representatives to be broken, the Federalist party came very near to making Burr the President, contrary to the wishes of the majority.

We the People *of the United States, in order to form a more perfect Union, establish insure domestic Tranquility, provide for the common defence, promote the general Welfare, and secure the Blessings of Liberty to and our Posterity, do ordain and establish this Constitution for the United States of America.*

Article I.

Representatives shall choose immediately, by ballot, the President. But in choosing the President, the votes shall be taken by states, the representation from each state having one vote; a quorum for this purpose shall consist of a member or members from two-thirds of the states, and a majority of all the states shall be necessary to a choice. And if the House of Representatives shall not choose a President, whenever the right of choice shall devolve upon them, before the fourth day of March next following, then the Vice-President shall act as President, as in case of the death or other constitutional disability of the President. The person having the greatest number of votes as Vice-President shall be the Vice-President, if such number be a majority of the whole number of electors appointed and if no person have a majority, then, from the two highest numbers on the list, the Senate shall choose the Vice-President; a quorum for the purpose shall consist of two-thirds of the whole number of Senators, and a majority of the whole number shall be necessary to a choice. But no person constitutionally ineligible to the office of President shall be eligible to that of Vice-President of the United States."

After this amendment, and under the traditions of the political parties, all members of the Electoral College now vote for a President and Vice-President exactly as the popular vote has demanded.

The Constitution had failed to say what should be done if a President had not been chosen by inauguration day. Nor had it stated the obvious fact that the Vice-President's qualifications should be the same as the President's. This amendment corrected those oversights.

You give: Provision for eliminating a tie vote between President and Vice-President.

You get: (*a*) Greater assurance that the voters' choice will become President; (*b*) removal of a possible source of bitter political conflict.

AMENDMENT 13
(Adopted in 1865)

SECTION 1

"Neither slavery nor involuntary servitude, except as a punishment for crime whereof the party shall have been duly convicted, shall exist within the United States, or any place subject to their jurisdiction."

SECTION 2

"Congress shall have power by appropriate legislation to enforce the provisions of this article."

Amendments 13, 14, and 15 resulted from the War Between the States. These amendments impose upon the states certain restrictions which are to be enforced by the federal government. Thus, they helped to settle one of the underlying causes of the war, that is, the power of the states versus the power of the federal government.

In 1863 President Lincoln issued the Emancipation Proclamation. As a clear statement of one thing the North was fighting for, the proclamation has become famous. But it had little practical effect. The actual freeing of the slaves occurred when Amendment 13 was adopted.

Involuntary servitude means about the same thing as slavery. In general, this amendment says that no one in the United States or its possessions may be made to work without wages or in confinement except as punishment for crime.

You give: (*a*) Instructions prohibiting slavery; (*b*) power to Congress to enforce that prohibition.

You get: Protection against enforced labor or confinement for every person, except a criminal, who is under the jurisdiction of the United States government.

AMENDMENT 14
(*Adopted in 1868*)
SECTION 1

"All persons born or naturalized in the United States, and subject to the jurisdiction thereof, are citizens of the United States and of the state wherein they reside."

"No state shall make or enforce any law which shall abridge the privileges or immunities of citizens of the United States, nor shall any state deprive any person of life, liberty, or property without due process of law, nor deny to any person within its jurisdiction the equal protection of the laws."

The primary intention of this section was to make the former slaves citizens and to protect their fundamental rights from any action by the states.

Because of later interpretations, the meaning has been so broadened that Section 1 is now one of the most important parts of the Constitution. It defines citizenship both in the United States and in the states. It also prohibits states from interfering with the privileges or immunities of United States citizens.

Most important are the words: "nor shall any state deprive any person of life, liberty, or property without due process of law." These words have come to mean: (1) That the states must follow fair, legal procedures when they try to take away a person's life, liberty, or property. For example, a man may not be abused to make him confess to a crime. (2) That in some instances states may not deprive persons of certain rights and privileges no matter how legal the procedure. The words are used, for example, to protect freedom of speech, press, and assembly from interference by the states.

The last words of this section mean that whatever privileges are given or regulations imposed must be extended equally to all persons to whom they apply.

AMENDMENT 14
SECTION 2

"Representatives shall be apportioned among the several states according to their respective numbers, counting the whole number of persons in each state, excluding Indians not taxed. But when the right to vote at any election for the choice of electors for President and Vice-President of the United States, Representatives in Congress, the executive and judicial officers of a state, or the members of the Legislature thereof, is denied to any of the male inhabitants of such state, being twenty-one years of age, and citizens of the United States, or in any way abridged, except for participation in rebellion, or other crime, the basis of representation therein shall be reduced in the proportion which the number of such male citizens shall bear to the whole number of male citizens twenty-one years of age in such state."

Prior to this amendment, only three-fifths of Negro slaves had been included in the population when membership in the House of Representatives was apportioned among the states. (See page 20.) Now, each male over twenty-one years of age, regardless of color, was to be counted.

The Republicans, who were in control of Congress when this amendment was adopted, realized that it would increase the number of Representatives from the Southern states, whose white population was solidly Democratic. Fearing this blow to their power in Congress, the Republicans tried to see to it that the freedmen, who were favorable to the Republican party, would be allowed to vote; or, if they were not, that the Southern states would be penalized by deducting the freedmen from the state population when membership in the House of Representatives was apportioned.

All states have laws which determine who may vote and who may not. Because most states might be subject to some penalty under this amendment, Congress has never attempted to apply it.

AMENDMENT 14
Section 3

"No person shall be a Senator or Representative in Congress, or elector of President and Vice-President, or hold any office, civil or military, under the United States, or under any state, who, having previously taken an oath, as a member of Congress, or as an officer of the United States, or as a member of any state Legislature, or as an executive or judicial officer of any state, to support the Constitution of the United States, shall have engaged in insurrection or rebellion against the same, or given aid or comfort to the enemies thereof. But Congress may, by a vote of two-thirds of each house, remove such disability."

*One nation,   indivisible, with liberty
and justice for all ..*

Many leaders of the Confederacy had previously been officials of the United States government or had held offices under state governments. When they took those positions they had sworn an oath to support the Constitution. It was now held that they had violated their oaths when they joined or aided the Confederate forces, and Congress set out to punish them by forbidding them to hold public office again.

The effect of this punishment was to deprive the South of most of its able leaders. After passing several acts applying to specific people, Congress passed a blanket act in 1872 removing the restriction from most of those who had served the Confederacy. In 1898 all others were finally pardoned.

AMENDMENT 14
Section 4

"The validity of the public debt of the United States, authorized by law, including debts incurred for payment of pensions and bounties for services in suppressing insurrection and rebellion, shall not be questioned. But neither the United States nor any state shall assume or pay any debt or obligation incurred in aid of insurrection or rebellion against the United States, or any claim for the loss or emancipation of any slave; but all such debts, obligations, and claims shall be held illegal and void."

Section 5

"The Congress shall have power to enforce, by appropriate legislation, the provisions of this article."

The first part of Section 4 was included so that Congressmen from the Southern states would not be tempted to pass laws denying payment of debts incurred by the United States government during the War Between the States. Further, it forbade the federal government and the state governments to pay any debts incurred in support of the Confederacy. Confederate bonds and money, of course, became worthless.

You give: (*a*) A clear definition of United States citizenship and state citizenship; (*b*) instructions that prevent state interference with certain basic rights.

You get: Assurance (*a*) that all who are entitled to citizenship will have it; (*b*) that if any state restricts certain fundamental rights of citizens or others, the federal government will step in to protect them.

AMENDMENT 15
(Adopted in 1870)
SECTION 1

"The right of the citizens of the United States to vote shall not be denied or abridged by the United States or by any state on account of race, color, or previous condition of servitude."

SECTION 2

"The Congress shall have power to enforce this article by appropriate legislation."

This amendment forbade the states, as well as the federal government, to restrict the right of a citizen to vote because of his color or race, or because he was once a slave. It did not permit all citizens to vote, for voting qualifications were left almost entirely to the states, subject to such restrictions as this. Nor did it extend the vote to women, who were not generally considered full-fledged citizens at this time (see page 245). It was, however, a long step forward in the principles of republican government.

You deny: To all governments within the United States the right to exclude or restrain anyone from voting because of his color, race, or previous status as a slave.

You get: Assurance that fewer restrictions will be placed on the right of citizens to vote.

AMENDMENT 16
(*Adopted in 1913*)

"The Congress shall have power to lay and collect taxes on incomes, from whatever source derived, without apportionment among the several states, and without regard to any census or enumeration."

Tax Collector

Amendment 16 was added to reverse a decision of the Supreme Court. The Constitution gives Congress the power to collect taxes subject to certain limitations (see pages 23, 64, and 98). One of these limitations is that direct taxes must be apportioned among the states according to population.

In 1894 Congress levied a tax on incomes. The following year the Supreme Court held the tax unconstitutional as applied to the income from various kinds of property because it was a direct tax and not apportioned according to population. This meant that the tax was almost totally ineffective, since most incomes large enough to be taxed came from stocks and bonds and other property.

Amendment 16 changes that decision of the Supreme Court by making it constitutional for Congress to tax incomes "from whatever source derived." Income taxes are now the major source of money for the federal government.

You give: The federal government power to tax all incomes.

You get: Money to operate the federal government.

AMENDMENT 17

(Adopted in 1913)

CLAUSE 1

"The Senate of the United States shall be composed of two Senators from each state, elected by the people thereof, for six years; and each Senator shall have one vote. The electors in each state shall have the qualifications requisite for electors of the most numerous branch of the state Legislatures."

CLAUSE 2

"When vacancies happen in the representation of any state in the Senate, the executive authority of such state shall issue writs of election to fill such vacancies: *Provided*, That the Legislature of any state may empower the executive thereof to make temporary appointments until the people fill the vacancies by election as the Legislature may direct."

CLAUSE 3

"This amendment shall not be so construed as to affect the election or term of any Senator chosen before it becomes valid as part of the Constitution."

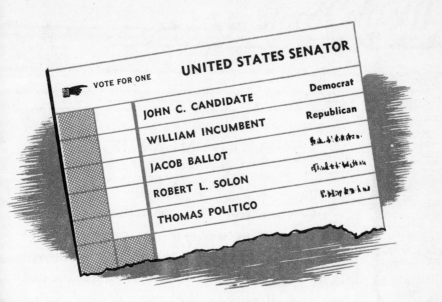

Until 1913, when this amendment was adopted, United States Senators were chosen by the state Legislatures, as specified in Article 1, Section 3, Clause 1 (page 28). Deadlocks and other delays in the Legislatures often left states without their full vote in the Senate. It was finally decided that Senators should be elected in the same way as Representatives.

You give: Instructions that Senators are to be elected directly by the voters.

You get: (*a*) A Senate more responsive to the needs of the people; (*b*) assurance that each state will have full representation in the Senate.

AMENDMENT 18
(*Adopted in 1919*)
SECTION 1

~~"After one year from the ratification of this article the manufacture, sale, or transportation of intoxicating liquors within, the importation thereof into, or the exportation thereof from the United States and all territory subject to the jurisdiction thereof for beverage purposes is hereby prohibited."~~

SECTION 2

~~"The Congress and the several states shall have concurrent power to enforce this article by appropriate legislation."~~

SECTION 3

~~"This article shall be inoperative unless it shall have been ratified as an amendment to the Constitution by the Legislatures of the several states, as provided in the Constitution, within seven years from the date of the submission hereof to the states by the Congress."~~

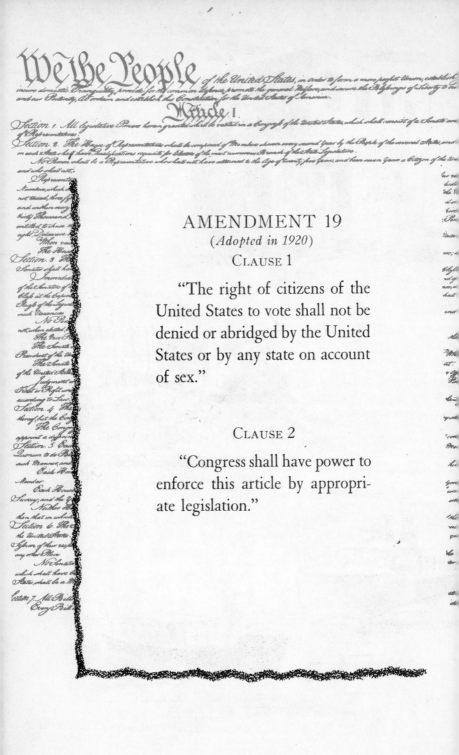

AMENDMENT 19
(*Adopted in 1920*)
Clause 1

"The right of citizens of the United States to vote shall not be denied or abridged by the United States or by any state on account of sex."

Clause 2

"Congress shall have power to enforce this article by appropriate legislation."

When the Constitution was written, women's opinions were not welcomed in public affairs, least of all in politics. During the 1800's, however, this attitude began to change. By the early 1900's, a number of states had amended their constitutions so that women could vote. Finally, in 1920, this amendment was adopted so that women throughout the United States could take part in state and national elections.

You deny: To the federal government and the state governments any right to prevent citizens from voting because of their sex.

You get: Participation of women in settling questions that affect all citizens.

AMENDMENT 20

(Adopted in 1933)

SECTION 1

"The terms of the President and Vice-President shall end at noon on the 20th day of January, and the terms of Senators and Representatives at noon on the 3d day of January, of the years in which such terms would have ended if this article had not been ratified; and the terms of their successors shall then begin."

SECTION 2

"The Congress shall assemble at least once in every year, and such meeting shall begin at noon on the 3d day of January, unless they shall by law appoint a different day."

SECTION 3

"If, at the time fixed for the beginning of the term of the President, the President-elect shall have died, the Vice-President-elect shall become President. If a President shall not have been chosen before the time fixed for the beginning of his term, or if the President-elect shall have failed to qualify, then the Vice-President-elect shall act as President until a President shall have qualified; and the Congress may by law provide for the case wherein

The main purpose of this amendment was
to cut down the interval between November of
one year, when the people elected a new President and new Congressmen, and March 4 of
the next year, when the new officials began their
terms in office. That interval was necessary when
the Constitution was written because communication and transportation were slow. In modern
times the delay was unnecessary. And it was
undesirable for two main reasons: (1) After the
voters had expressed their choice of a President,
they had to wait more than four months for him
to start doing the things they wanted him to
do. Meantime, the outgoing President, having
lost the confidence of the people, found it difficult to carry out his duties. (2) Newly elected
Congressmen began their terms on March 4, but
did not start making laws until December of the
year after they were elected (see page 44).
Thus, unless a special session of Congress were
called, thirteen months would pass before they
could begin doing what they had been elected

neither a President-elect nor a Vice-President-elect shall have qualified, declaring who shall then act as President, or the manner in which one who is to act shall be selected, and such person shall act accordingly until a President or Vice-President shall have qualified."

SECTION 4

"The Congress may by law provide for the case of the death of any of the persons from whom the House of Representatives may choose a President whenever the right of choice shall have devolved upon them, and for the case of the death of any of the persons from whom the Senate may choose a Vice-President whenever the right of choice shall have devolved upon them."

SECTION 5

"Sections 1 and 2 shall take effect on the 15th day of October following the ratification of this article."

SECTION 6

"This article shall be inoperative unless it shall have been ratified as an amendment to the Constitution by the Legislatures of three-fourths of the several states within seven years from the date of its submission."

to do. Meantime, from December of election year until March 4 of the following year, the old Congress continued to sit. Included in it were Senators and Representatives whom the people had already turned down at the polls. If there were many of them, as sometimes happened, they could delay important laws in order to embarrass their successors, or even pass laws contrary to the wishes which voters had expressed in the election. Such Congressmen were called "lame ducks."

Amendment 20, sometimes called "The Lame Duck Amendment," streamlined this procedure. Newly elected Congressmen begin work now on January 3, about a month and a half after election, and the new President takes office on January 20.

Amendment 20 also outlines what shall be done if a newly elected President or Vice-President should die or fail to qualify before taking office. It also specifies what shall be done if a candidate dies while a close election is being settled in Congress (see pages 222–24).

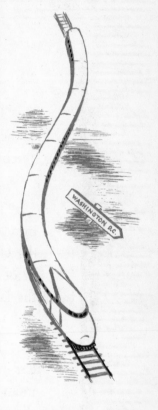

You give: Instructions (*a*) which allow your elected representatives to start carrying out your wishes soon after election; (*b*) which remove from defeated representatives any power to obstruct your wishes.

You get: A national government more responsive to public opinion and to the will of the people.

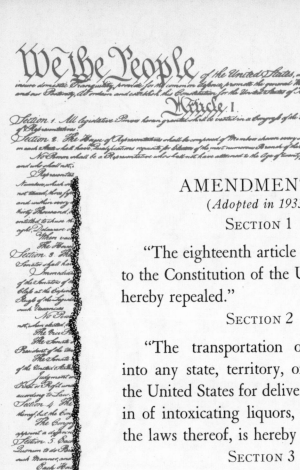

AMENDMENT 21
(Adopted in 1933)

SECTION 1

"The eighteenth article of amendment to the Constitution of the United States is hereby repealed."

SECTION 2

"The transportation or importation into any state, territory, or possession of the United States for delivery or use therein of intoxicating liquors, in violation of the laws thereof, is hereby prohibited."

SECTION 3

"This article shall be inoperative unless it shall have been ratified as an amendment to the Constitution by convention in the several states, as provided in the Constitution, within seven years from the date of the submission hereof to the states by the Congress."

Amendment 18, the Prohibition Amendment, was repealed. Section 2, however, protects any state that wants to continue prohibition.

HOUSE COMPLETED

YOUR
HOUSE
OF
FREEDOM

The Constitution of the United States, with
the Bill of Rights and the other amendments,
is the blueprint for your House of Freedom.

The government of the United States is the construction organization commissioned by you to build your House of Freedom. Within that organization there are three main branches.

Representative

Senator

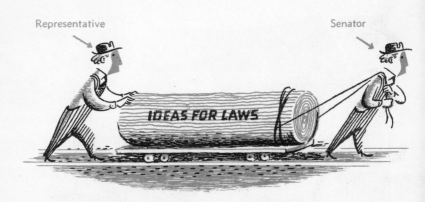

The people elected by you to operate the sawmills and furnish materials for the framework are the first branch. They are the members of Congress, who make the federal laws.

**1. THE LEGISLATIVE BRANCH
OF THE UNITED STATES GOVERNMENT**

ESTABLISH JUSTICE,

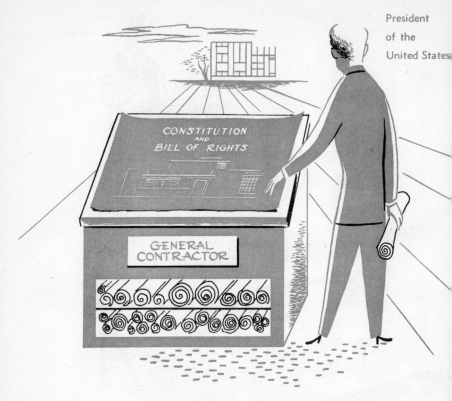

**2. THE EXECUTIVE BRANCH
OF THE UNITED STATES GOVERNMENT**

The second branch includes the President of
the United States and all the people who work
with him. It is the President's job to see that
the building goes up according to specifications.
He is the contractor in charge of construction.

INSURE DOMESTIC TRANQUILITY,

**3. THE JUDICIAL BRANCH
OF THE UNITED STATES GOVERNMENT**

Building inspectors make certain that the contractor is following the plans and that the right materials are going into the house. These inspectors, the third branch, are the members of the Supreme Court of the United States.

PROVIDE FOR THE COMMON DEFENSE,

Your House of Freedom rests on a foundation made of two materials: (1) respect for the guiding principles of the American form of government; (2) voluntary obedience to the laws.

Through the years, most American citizens have respected the government and obeyed the laws of the United States. Thus, your House of Freedom has stood firm through wars, depressions, and other kinds of national crises.

PROMOTE THE GENERAL WELFARE,

The plans for your House of Freedom call for openings in the foundation. The fresh air of public opinion enters these openings and circulates within the framework of the building.

The fresh air of public opinion keeps out dry rot that might weaken the framework of the House of Freedom. Good citizens constantly follow the affairs of the government so that their opinions will be thoughtful and intelligent.

AND SECURE THE BLESSINGS OF LIBERTY

The laws of the United States are the framework of your House of Freedom. These laws are made by the Legislative Branch, enforced and carried out by the Executive Branch, inspected and interpreted by the Judicial Branch. Study the framework. See how it is put together.

TO OURSELVES AND OUR POSTERITY,

It would be a poor kind of house in which some of the nails failed to do their jobs. In the United States, people of all races and creeds vote and carry out other duties of citizenship. The people are the nails that hold together the framework of your House of Freedom.

DO ORDAIN AND ESTABLISH

So—Your House of Freedom is built . . .

The logs have been cut.

The construction has been supervised.

The building and materials
have been inspected.

THIS CONSTITUTION

Now—What is its cost?

The cost of your House of Freedom is respect for the government, obedience to its laws, thoughtful opinions, and participation in the duties of citizenship. In return for these payments, the deed to the house becomes yours.

FOR THE UNITED STATES OF AMERICA.

Deed

This Indenture, BETWEEN YOU, A CITIZEN, AND THE UNITED STATES OF AMERICA,

Witnesseth: THAT IN RETURN FOR RESPECT TOWARD THE GOVERN-MENT, OBEDIENCE TO ITS LAWS, THOUGHTFUL OPINIONS, AND PAR-TICIPATION IN THE DUTIES OF CITIZENSHIP, YOU ARE GRANTED A HOUSE OF FREEDOM, TO HAVE AND TO HOLD, TOGETHER WITH PRO-TECTION OF YOUR LIFE, LIBERTY, AND PROPERTY,

Upon Your Agreement: THAT YOU WILL KEEP YOUR HOUSE IN GOOD CONDITION AND REPAIR.

In Witness Whereof: WE SET OUR HANDS AND SEALS.

Uncle Sam

_____
YOUR SIGNATURE

[267]

Among the important guaranties in the deed to your House of Freedom are these:

✓ The protection of a written Constitution which is the supreme law of the land (page 184).

✓ A peaceful, lawful means of amending the Constitution (pages 171–79).

✓ An energetic system of government capable of meeting your needs.

✓ A system of checks and balances among the various departments of the government.

✓ Protection against foreign invasion and domestic violence (page 168).

✓ A republican form of government in your state (page 168).

✓ Free movement among the states and the same privileges and immunities in all the states (page 160).

✓ The right to vote regardless of race or sex (pages 236, 244).

✓ The right to hold any public office for which you are qualified.

IN YOUR DEED

✓ Freedom of religion, speech, press, assembly, and petition (page 196).

✓ Protection against unreasonable searches and seizures of your person or property (page 202).

✓ Just compensation for any property taken from you for public use (page 204).

✓ Protection against being deprived of your life, liberty, or property without due process of law (pages 204, 228).

✓ Freedom from slavery or involuntary servitude except as punishment for crime (page 226).

✓ Equal protection of the laws (page 228).

✓ Protection from bills of attainder and ex post facto laws (page 96).

✓ Protection against being held in jail indefinitely without a trial (page 94).

✓ Established procedures to protect your rights when you are accused of crime (pages 150, 204, 206).

✓ In criminal cases, the right to a speedy public trial by jury (page 150); in civil cases, a trial by jury if you want it (page 208).

FREEDOM THE BEST FOR YOU

INDEX

ARTICLES, SECTIONS, AND CLAUSES

INDEX TO SUBJECTS

Citizens: abroad, 83; controversies between, 146, 147, 220, 221; defined, 228, 229; drafted into armed forces, 87; qualified for office, 18, 19, 32, 33, 118, 119; of states, 160–61, 228, 229; through naturalization, 74, 75; voting rights of, 230, 231, 236–37, 244–45

City governments: laws of, 185; powers assigned to, 217

Civil rights. *See* Bill of Rights

Civil Service Commission, 134

Claims: for loss or emancipation of slaves, 234, 235; nothing in Constitution to prejudice, 166

Coin: foreign, regulation of value of, 76; gold and silver, 104; punishment for counterfeiting of, 78, 79; and states, 104

Coining of money: forbidden states, 104, 105; and power of Congress, 76, 77

Colonists, and quartering of soldiers, 201

Color, and restriction of suffrage, 236, 237

Commander in chief, 85, 126, 127, 128, 129

Commerce: equality of regulations of, 100, 101; with foreign nations, 70, 71, 72, 93, 101; with Indian tribes, 70, 73; interference with, 73; interstate, 70, 71, 72–73, 93, 100, 101, 107; between states and foreign nations, 107

Commissions: of all officers of the United States, 136, 138, 139; granted during recess of Senate, 130, 133

Common defense, 6, 8, 64, 66

Common law: re-examination of facts according to rules of, 208, 209; suits at, 208, 209

Communication: better systems of, 79; laws governing, 71

Compact. *See* Agreement

Compensation: of Congressmen, 50, 51; of Judges, 144, 145; of President, 122–23; for private property, 204, 205

Compulsory process, for obtaining witnesses, 206, 207

Concurrent power, of Congress and the several states, 242

Confederacy: bonds of, 235; office denied to leaders of, 232, 233

Confederation, prohibited states, 104, 105

Confession, in open court, 152

Congress: all legislative powers vested in, 14–17, 145; election to, 42–43, 46; organization of, 44–50, 56–63, 136, 139, 246; powers and duties of, 20, 21–22, 23, 48, 49, 64–93, 99, 118, 130, 132–33, 135, 144, 148, 150, 154–55, 158–59, 164–67, 172, 174, 179, 226, 232–34, 236, 238–39, 242, 244; public records of, 49; restrictions upon, 53, 94–95, 102, 103, 133, 196, 197; and states, 106–9; and succession to presidency, 120–21, 246, 248, 249

Congressmen: compensation of, 50, 51; election of, 42–43; freedom of, from arrest, 50, 51; as lawmakers, 17, 256; may not hold civil office, 52, 53; qualified, 49; voted out of office, 17, 55

Conservation of natural resources, 72

Constitution of states: under Articles of Confederation, 216; bills of rights in, 217

Constitution of the United States: basis of, 216; debts incurred before adoption of, 182, 183; oath of allegiance to, 186, 187; ordained and established, 6, 9; powers vested by, 92, 93, 216; ratification of, 189–92; and reserved powers, 214, 216; retainment of rights by, 212–13; signers of, 190–91; states under, 7; as supreme law, 184, 192; what it does, 4; written, 2

Constitutional Convention, 2, 21, 173, 190

Constitutionality, judicial interpretation of, 145

Consuls. *See* Ambassadors

Contracts, obligation of, 104, 105

Controversies, judicial power over, 146, 147

Conventions: of political parties, 117; for proposing amendments, 172, 174, 175; for ratification of amendments, 172, 174, 175; for ratification of Constitution, 190, 192, 193

Conviction of treason, 152, 153

Copyright, 80, 81

Corruption of blood, 154

Counsel for defense, rights to, 206, 207

Counterfeiting, punishment for, 78, 79

County governments: laws of, 185; powers assigned to, 217

Courthouses, owned by United States government, 91

Courts: and appointment of inferior officers, 130; federal, 82, 83, 144, 145, 147, 148, 208, 209, 220–21; and re-examination of facts, 208, 209; regular procedure of, 41

Credit: bills of, forbidden to states, 104; interstate, of state proceedings, 158–59; of the United States, 68

Crime: capital or other infamous, 204, 205; high, impeachment for, 140–41; in meaning of Constitution, 151; trial of, 150–51, 206, 207

Customs officials, appointment of, 133

Death, and succession to presidency, 120–21, 246, 248

Debate, Congressmen free from question concerning, 50, 51

Debts: incurred in aid of insurrection or rebellion, 234, 235; incurred under Articles of Confederation, 182–83; incurred in struggle for independence, 183; of an individual, 75; payment of, 64, 66, 67, 104; validity of, affirmed, 182, 183, 234, 235

Defense, in trials, 206, 207; *see also* Common defense

Delegated powers: of federal government, 93, 216, 217; of state governments, 216, 217

·Departments of government, powers of, 92; *see also* Executive departments

Dictatorship, 5

Direct election, of Senators, 240, 241; *see also* Popular election

Direct tax: apportionment of, 20, 23, 65; on buildings or land, 99; on incomes, 99; on persons, 99; prohibited unless in proportion to census, 98–99; unpopular and unfair, 99

Disability, removal of, 120

Discoveries, exclusive right to, 80–81

Discussion, of Constitution, 192, 193

Disorderly behavior, 48, 49

Disqualification, in cases of impeachment, 40

District, wherein a crime is committed, 206

District courts, and federal cases, 149

District of Columbia: exclusive legislation over, 90–91; governed by board of commissioners, 91; as seat of government, 90–91

Division: of Congress into two houses, 17; of powers, 4, 5, 185; of Senators into three classes, 30

Dockyards, property of the United States, 90

Domestic tranquility, 6, 8

Domestic violence, protection of states from, 168, 169

Draft, of citizens into the armed forces, 87

Due process of law, 204, 205, 228, 229

Duties: power to levy, 64, 65, 67, 72; restriction upon states to levy, 100, 106–7

"Elastic clause," 92–93

Election: campaign, 43; of Congress, 42–43, 46, 47; direct, *see* Direct election; popular, *see* Popular election; of President and Vice-President, 114–18, 222–25; of Representatives, 18, 19, 25; of Senators, 28, 240, 241

Electoral College, 115, 117, 223, 225

Electors: appointment of, 114; choice of, 117, 118; and participation in rebellion, 232, 233; for President and Vice-President, 114–15, 117, 118, 222, 223; for Representatives, 18, 19; for Senators, 240

Emancipation Proclamation, 227

Emoluments: from foreign powers, 50–53, 102, 103; beyond regular compensation, forbidden to President, 122

Enforcement: of amendments, 226, 234, 236, 242, 244; of laws, 136, 138, 139

Enumeration: of certain rights in Constitution, 212, 213; power to tax without regard to, 238–39

Equity, 146, 147

Evidence, inadequate, 209

Ex post facto laws: defined, 97; prohibited to national government, 96, 97; prohibited to states, 104

Excise, power to levy, 64, 65, 67

Execution of laws, 136, 138, 139

Executive authority, of state, 24, 30, 162, 168, 240

Executive branch, 5, 15, 111–41, 258

Executive departments. *See* Cabinet

Executive officers, and oath to support Constitution, 186, 187

Executive powers, vested in President, 112, 113, 128

Exemptions, of Congressmen, from arrest, 50

Expenditures, 102, 103

Export: duties on, prohibited to states, 106, 107; of intoxicating liquors, 242, 243; of materials needed at home, 72; tax on, *see* Export tax

Export tax, on articles from any state, forbidden, 100, 101

Express companies, and interstate commerce, 72

Expulsion of Congressmen, 48, 49

Extradition, 162–63

Facts: establishment of, 209; function of jury to decide, 151; re-examination of, 208, 209

Faith, interstate, 158–59

Federal courts. *See* Courts

Federal government: authority of, 90, 185; and Bill of Rights, 193; laws and treaties of, 185; powers of, 4, 212, 213, 214–17; restrictions upon, 196, 217

Federal Reserve Board, appointment of members of, 133

Felonies: power to define and punish, 82, 83; and privileges of members of Congress, 50

Fines, excessive, prohibited in Bill of Rights, 210, 211

First Congress, and Bill of Rights, 193

Foreign-born persons, and citizenship, 75; *see also* Naturalization

Foreign states: agreement with, 108, 109; commerce with, 70, 71, 72, 93, 101, 107; disputes with, 83; and judicial power of United States, 146, 147, 220, 221; presents from, 102

Forests: owned by United States government, 91; power to regulate, 167

Forts, 90

Franklin, Benjamin, 2

Freedom: of press, 196, 197; of religion, 196, 197; of speech, 196, 197

Fugitive, from justice, 162–63

Fugitive slaves, 164

General welfare: promotion of, 6, 8; provision for, 64, 66

Gold and silver. *See* Coin

Good behavior, and terms of judges, 144

Goods: control over, entering or leaving country, 71; free flow of, 73

Government: based on separation of powers, 5; characteristics of, 169; as federal sys-

Order: of laws, 185; obligation to maintain, 83
Orders, and approval by President, 62
Original jurisdiction, of Supreme Court, 148, 149
Overt act, and conviction of treason, 152

Pardons and reprieves, 126
Parks: owned by United States government, 91; power to regulate, 167
Parties, political, 25; development of, 117; and selection of candidates, 117, 223
Passage of bills, 56
Patents, 80–81
Peace, time of, 108, 200
Pensions, 234
People: powers reserved to, 214–17; rights retained by, 212–13
Petition, right to, 196, 197
Piracy, 82, 83
Popular election, 19, 23; of President and Vice-President, 115, 117, 225; see also Direct election
Population, 20, 21, 22, 23, 29, 99
Port of New York Authority, 109
Ports, equality of, 100, 101
Possessions, of the United States, 242, 250
Post offices: owned by United States government, 91; power to establish, 78, 79
Post roads, power to establish, 78, 79
Posterity, 6, 9
Postmasters, appointment of, 133
Poverty, utter, protection from, 75
Powers: delegated, 93, 216, 217; division of, 4, 5, 185; executive, 112, 113, 118; judicial, 146–47, 220–21; legislative, 14–17, 24, 26, 42, 64; political, 216, 217; reserved, 214, 215, 216, 217; sovereign, 3, 4, 169
Preference, to ports, prohibited, 100, 101
Presentment. See Indictment
Presents, from foreign powers, 102
Presidency, succession to. See Succession
President of the Senate, 34, 114, 116, 117, 222
President of the United States: compensation of, 122–23; election of, 114–18, 222–25; executive power vested in, 112, 113; oath of, 124–25; powers and duties of, 45, 56, 57; 60–63, 85, 91, 126–39, 145, 258; qualifications of, 118, 119, 246, 248; removal of, by impeachment, 38, 39, 120, 140–41; succession to office of, see Succession; term of, 112, 246
President pro tempore of Senate, 121
Press, freedom of, 196, 197, 229
Prince, and officers of the United States, 102
Priority of supreme law, 185
Privacy, 201, 203
Privileges: of citizens, 160–61, 228, 229; of copyright, 81; and loyalty to Constitution, 187; of members of Congress, 50, 51
Procedure, with bills, 54–63

Proceedings: journal of, 48; rules of, 48, 49
Profit, office of, 102, 103, 114
Progress, promotion of, 80
Prohibition: of intoxicating liquors, 242–43, 250–51; of powers, 214–17
Property: private, 202–5, 228, 229; of the United States, 90, 91, 166–67
Prosecutions, criminal, 206, 207
Protection, 27, 67, 72, 153, 161, 165, 167; of citizens, 73, 75, 83, 155, 201, 202–3, 228–29; of states, 101, 168, 169, 220–21
Public acts. See Acts
Public safety, 94
Punishment: for counterfeiting, 78, 79; cruel and unusual, prohibited, 210, 211; for disorderly behavior, 48; for impeachment, 40, 41; for insurrection or rebellion, 232, 233; of lawbreakers, 163; for treason, 154–55

Qualifications: judgment of, 46, 47; of the President, 118, 119, 246, 248; and religious test, 186, 187; of Representatives, 18, 19; of Senators, 32, 33
Quartering of soldiers, 200–201
Questioning: of Congressmen, 50; of validity of public debt, 234
Quorum, 46, 116, 224

Race, and restriction of suffrage, 236, 237
Railroads, and interstate commerce, 72
Ratification: of amendments, 193, 242, 248, 250; of Constitution, 189–92
Rebellion: debts incurred in, 234, 235; payment for services in suppressing, 234, 235; punishment for, 232–33; and suspension of writ of habeas corpus, 94–95
Receipts and expenditures, regular statement of, 102, 103
Recess of Senate, filling of vacancies during, 130–31
Recommendation of measures, power of President in, 136
Reconstruction amendment, 228–35
Records, interstate credit of, 158–59
Redress of grievances, 196, 197
Regulation of commerce or revenue, 100, 101
Religion: freedom of, 196, 197; as test for office, 186, 187
Removal from office, by impeachment, 38, 39, 120, 140–41
Repeal of Amendment 18, 250–51
Representation, 20, 22, 28, 29, 230
Representatives: apportionment of, 20, 22, 29, 230; bound by oath to support Constitution, 186, 187; compensation of, 50, 51; death or resignation of, 25; election of, 18, 19, 25, 42, 43, 46, 241; and participation in rebellion, 232–33; privileges of, 50, 51; qualifications of, 18, 19, 46; restrictions upon, 52, 53, 114; term of, 18, 19, 246

Date Due